The *Cogito* in
Husserl's Philosophy

Northwestern University
STUDIES IN *Phenomenology &*
Existential Philosophy

Gaston Berger

Translated by

With an Introduction by

The *Cogito* in Husserl's Philosophy

KATHLEEN McLAUGHLIN

JAMES M. EDIE

NORTHWESTERN UNIVERSITY PRESS

EVANSTON   1 9 7 2

Contents

Introduction

PHENOMENOLOGY, AS A DEVELOPING CURRENT in contemporary philosophy, is now at a crossroads; its form and content are taking directions which its founder, Edmund Husserl,
could never have foreseen and at some of which he would be ap-
palled. The *early phenomenological movement* was based on the
highly selected and incomplete sample of his writings which
Husserl published during his own lifetime. A number of his
disciples, like Fink, Landgrebe, Gurwitsch, Stein, and some of his
collaborators on his *Jahrbuch,* have produced commentaries on
his thought which are quite strictly according to his own spirit.
But it was the dissident disciples, like Scheler, Pfänder, Ingarden,
and Heidegger, who achieved the greater notoriety and who had
the greater immediate success, particularly in Germany. By the
early 1930's Husserl's own thought had already been "drowned
in silence" [1] and, thanks to this silence, was replaced, even before
the war, by existentialism. If we divide the available commentaries on Husserl's thought into three broad categories, it is the
early period which is the most sparsely represented.

The existential interpretation given to Husserl's thought in
France and Belgium after the Second World War, particularly
by Sartre, Merleau-Ponty, De Waelhens, and Ricoeur (often called
"the second school of phenomenology"), coincided historically
with the gradual publication of his *Nachlass* at Louvain, the
translation of his major works into English and other Western
languages, and with the gradual diffusion of his thought through-

1. Pierre Thévenaz, in *What Is Phenomenology?*, ed. James M. Edie
(Chicago: Quadrangle Books, 1962), p. 40. During the Nazi period, Husserl, when he was referred to at all by contemporary German philosophers,
was treated as "an obscure Jewish mystic" (*ibid.*, p. 171).

out the world. An accent was given to Husserlian phenomenology and to phenomenological research in general during these years which greatly influenced the manner in which Husserl's texts were read, how they were rated, and how they could be fruitfully interpreted so as to be of relevance to contemporary philosophical concerns. Phenomenology became Existential Phenomenology.

Now, particularly in the English-speaking world, phenomenology is undergoing a transformation. Though it is evident to anyone who reads the philosophical journals that phenomenology, and particularly Husserlian phenomenology, is a matter of great excitement and continuing philosophical interest, a new attitude is evident in the recent work of such young commentators as Mohanty, Sokolowski, Føllesdal, Dreyfus, and others. While there are still eminent representatives of "early" phenomenology among us, and a much greater and more diverse company of existential interpreters, the most recent work in phenomenology is addressed more and more to the predominant concerns of contemporary analytical and linguistic philosophy, to such an extent that the supposedly rigid methodological distinctions between these two enterprises is being blurred to the point of disappearance.

AMERICAN PHENOMENOLOGY, then, facing this conflict of interpretations, is in a reflective and pensive mood. It is taking stock of its past in an attitude of rigorous philosophical criticism. One feels that what was never a unified movement will become less so, that radical transformations are in the offing. Phenomenology is in a mood to become creative once again. We are now not only carefully assessing the works and intentions of the European fathers but are also reworking the various more or less conflicting interpretations which have been given to the original corpus. This is, therefore, a happy juncture at which to present to the American philosophical public the distinctive commentary on Husserl's work which Gaston Berger published in 1941. Though it comes from France, it is pre-existentialist in spirit and can be profitably read alongside of and in contrast to the better-known commentaries on Husserl by philosophers like Merleau-Ponty and Ricoeur.[2] It breathes an earlier, more rationalistic,

2. See Maurice Merleau-Ponty, *The Primacy of Perception*, ed. James M. Edie (Evanston: Northwestern University Press, 1964), especially the

almost Augustinian air. It is not my purpose here either to vindicate the validity of Berger's interpretation (in fact I disagree on a number of points, which I will not mention) or to advertise it as particularly authentic. But it is always useful, when one school of interpretation is in the ascendancy, to remind ourselves that there are other alternatives, whether we find them momentarily congenial or not.

Berger's interpretation of Husserl will be particularly congenial to all those who were introduced to philosophy through Cartesian rationalism or "the philosophy of the spirit"—a vague but accurate term used to designate the philosophical tradition which flows from Descartes and Malebranche, through Maine de Biran. to Lequier, Lavelle, Le Senne, Blondel, Thévénaz, and whatever proponents of *l'analyse réflexive* may still be among us.

Berger's *The* Cogito *in Husserl's Philosophy* has held for some time among phenomenologists the place of one of the "minor classics" of Husserlian interpretation; it is one of the most systematic and authoritative of the early commentaries, yet it had little sequel either in Berger's own work or in that of his associates and followers. It was published in the same year as his *grande thèse, Recherches sur les conditions de la connaissance,* which he defended at Aix before Maurice Blondel, Joseph Segond, and Jacques Paliard in 1941.[3]

The fall of France had already occurred, and Berger was at the time one of the *responsables* (from his "little house in the

essay on "Phenomenology and the Sciences of Man"; see also Paul Ricoeur, *Husserl: An Analysis of His Phenomenology,* trans. Edward G. Ballard and Lester E. Embree (Evanston: Northwestern University Press, 1967).

3. A complete bibliography of Berger's writings is appended to this volume. I have taken most of the biographical material mentioned in this essay from the commemorative volume of the journal *Les Etudes philosophiques* (Vol. XVI, No. 4, 1961), which appeared *in memoriam* the year following his death. At the defense of his thesis Léon Brunschvicg was present in the hall but asked Berger not to call attention to him for fear that the representative of the Vichy government who was presiding over the session would not recognize his right to speak, he being a Jew. After the defense, Brunschvicg is said to have spoken but one sentence to Berger: "You have proven as little as possible; you have only established those points which prove themselves." This was meant and accepted as high praise. Cf. Henry Duméry, "La Théorétique," *Les Etudes philosophiques,* XVI (1961), 362.

Alps" at Pierrevert in Haute-Provence) of the Resistance in south-eastern France.[4] Before becoming a professor of philosophy at Aix, he had been an industrialist in Marseilles; and then, from shortly after the end of the war until the time of his sudden death (in an automobile accident on November 13, 1960, at the age of sixty-four), he served the French government in several high administrative posts, most notably in the office of La Direction générale de l'Enseignement supérieur. There is no doubt that he had a flair for administration and that he enjoyed the opportunity this appointment gave him to "administer the universities" and "to organize intellectual cooperation," as he put it, by influencing the direction of scientific research. He organized the Fulbright Scholarship program in France and presided over the Institut International de Philosophie as well as numerous other national and international philosophical societies; and, in 1957, he founded the Centre International de Prospective, whose purpose was to bring together the intellectual elite, the inventors, the creators from all the professions (high government administrators, industrialists, managers, economists, doctors, psychologists, university professors, writers, and scientists) in order to foresee and to influence, if not to plan, the future development of human societies. It was because of his irrepressible social consciousness ("without an ethics . . . metaphysics loses all interest") [5] and his own primarily spiritual interests that (apart from his works on philosophical psychology and characterology, which do not concern us here) most of his later and more mature philosophical work took the form of occasional essays, addresses to learned societies and conferences, and short monographs on ethical subjects (solitude, friendship, courage, lucidity, detachment, sacrifice, sanctity).

Though he profoundly believed that "philosophy is the one serious thing," [6] his practical administrative responsibilities, which kept him to a strict timetable and an order of priorities

4. Henry Duméry, op. cit., p. 349.

5. Gaston Berger, "De la contradiction à l'inspiration," Les Etudes philosophiques, X (1955), 421.

6. Words from his opening discourse to the IX° Congrès des Sociétés de Philosophie de langue française (September 2, 1957), as quoted by Roger Mucchielli, "La Philosophie et la vie," Les Etudes philosophiques, XVI (1961), 364.

(hence his love and cultivation of "solitude" in the midst of activity), prevented him from a systematic development of his early work on Husserl. A number of his occasional essays from 1955–60 are concerned with the problem of time, and the book he was working on at the time of his death, *Phénoménologie du temps,* would have been the first major systematic sequel to his analysis of Husserl's notion of the *cogito* presented here.

WHAT WE HAVE HERE, then, is a pioneering work on Husserl's thought whose distinctive interpretation has not been followed up. Berger was, to all intents and purposes, the first French philosopher to take up Husserl's thought in a serious manner. His first Husserlian study is dated 1929, and a number of others, including the famous article "Husserl et Hume," appeared before he had completed his doctoral dissertation in 1941. The present book, particularly in its bibliographical data and in its reading of Husserl's posthumous *Nachlass,* is perforce somewhat out of date. Many of the most important essays cited, particularly those by Sartre, Fink, and Levinas, are now available, or will soon be available, in English, and the present state of our knowledge of Husserl's texts is considerably more advanced than that possessed by Berger.

It is all the more remarkable, therefore, and a sign of his penetration into the texts of Husserl available to him, that his reading of phenomenology strikes us today as completely fresh and stimulating. His selective repetition (*Wiederholung*—in the sense of "taking up again" in order to think-through-anew) of certain Husserlian themes is still useful even for those who know the whole historical record and have before them all the volumes of the *Husserliana* series. It is, in short, *a good introduction* to phenomenology, something we are still in need of even seventy years after the foundation of phenomenology.

Berger's book is centered around three interrelated themes, the *theory of intentionality,* the *theory of constitution,* and the *theory of evidence,* as these are developed in the major works Husserl published during his lifetime.

In these few introductory remarks I will limit myself to accentuating the special reading Berger gives to these themes in his development of them. It is the *theory of constitution* which is central. Berger treats it more thoroughly and with a greater sense of assurance than most commentators; this is surely one of the greatest merits of his book. He is one of the few commentators on Husserl to insist on Husserl's own fully explicit mistrust of ordinary language to describe the structures of transcendental consciousness. As Husserl tells us in the *Cartesian Meditations:* "Owing to the instability and ambiguity of common language and its much too great complacency about completeness of expression," phenomenology requires, "even when we use its means of expression," that there be a "legitimation" of the words used in terms of the ultimate "insights" which provide the "evidence" for the "significations" which the words we use express.[7] Berger thus begins by calling attention to "the mobility of vocabulary" (p. 53)—to the fact that Husserl does not completely fix the sense of his words or bind even his technical expressions with fixed and irrevocable definitions. That would be, Berger tells us, to take a naïvely dogmatic position with respect to the structures of experience—a position which phenomenology would find "much too sure of the future" to be able to claim to justify.

Berger emphasizes that, prior to the elaboration of any theory, Husserl simply wanted *to see*—and to describe what he saw.[8] Thus, in describing what he saw, Husserl used the phrases and expressions of ordinary language which seemed to him most suggestive and appropriate. His words serve only the function of turning us toward the primary preverbal structures, which we must grasp "in themselves." Thus, the fluidity of the language which Husserl uses to explain the constitution of objects should not be excessively worrisome if, through it, we are able to grasp what he means to say. Husserl variously speaks of the constitution of objects by consciousness as "creative," as a "productive

7. Edmund Husserl, *Cartesian Meditations,* trans. Dorion Cairns (The Hague: Nijhoff, 1960), pp. 13–14. This was a familiar theme of Husserl's. Cf. the remarks on the dangerous "seduction of language" in *The Crisis of European Sciences and Transcendental Phenomenology,* trans. David Carr (Evanston: Northwestern University Press, 1970), pp. 361–62.

8. Henry Duméry tells us that this was also characteristic of Berger. He was the kind of philosopher who, while not indifferent to logical relationships and purely conceptual questions, wanted above all *to see.* "His favorite question was not 'why,' or 'how,' but 'what is it' " (Henry Duméry, *op. cit.,* p. 350). We might compare this further to Wittgenstein's famous exhortation: "Don't think. Look!"

action," as an "active realization," as a "making," as an "operation" and an "actualization" (pp. 77–78). But, if we recognize that Husserl has no concern to unify his vocabulary and that his words are meant to suggest and point to, rather than to define, the absolute character of transcendental subjectivity, we will see that these expressions should not be taken literally. Strictly speaking, transcendental consciousness does not "make" anything; it is "neither receptive nor productive," writes Berger (p. 78).

What, then, is it? And how is it discovered and described? Transcendental constituting consciousness (what Husserl calls the "transcendental ego" as opposed to the "empirical ego") is the originary and absolute relationship of the I to the world and to all objects in the world; it is the relationship of having "objects." Transcendental phenomenology does not in any way deny the true existence of the world, which always continues to be experienced even within the reduction; its sole task is to turn from the factual world to the *sense* of this world of objects as it is experienced. "To grasp the constitution of the world by the ego . . . [is] a matter of seeing how the I gives a *sense* to everything presented to us in the world . . ." (p. 74).

Phenomenology is not the only current of philosophy to define philosophy as a turning-away from the empirical things and events in the real world toward the *meaning* of these "facts" and "states of affairs." But it is distinctive of phenomenology to relate all things and events, all facts and states of affairs—all "objects," in short—to a logically prior conscious activity which "unifies," "objectifies," and "identifies" its objects through time. Without consciousness in this fundamental sense of the experienced and selective activity of entertaining "objects" through time, there would be neither "objects" nor "world" (i.e., the ultimate unified system of the laws of the possible appearances of any conceivable meant objects).

What phenomenology accomplishes, then, in its turn to the foundations is to show that *the turn to meaning* involves ("implies") a turn to the transcendental subjectivity which alone can *mean,* and to see that transcendental subjectivity is the necessary and sufficient prior condition of there being any meant objects (i.e., a unified "world") at all. The turn to meaning involves us in a turn to the "meant objects" and the correlative "acts" of intending these objects that absolutely cannot be escaped. "Hence," writes Berger, "we must cease—and this is not easy—implicitly presupposing under meanings 'things' capable of supporting them and which consciousness would later make intelligible by applying to them its own form" (p. 75). Unlike the Neo-Kantians, Husserl's theory of constitution does not involve a quasi-cosmological "informing" of real things-in-themselves in the real empirical world with the mind's own prefabricated ideal "meanings" or "forms." Phenomenological reflection takes place wholly within the realm of "the meant"; it is a purely a priori study of eidetic meaning-relationships which takes place in complete independence of the existentially and factually real world, and yet this reflection does not involve philosophy in anything like a subjective or romanticist "idealism," precisely because the phenomenological *epoché* does not in any way challenge, deny, or even doubt the reality of the world. What it does is to discover and explicate the status and structures of "objectivity." Since there are "past objects," "imagined objects," "unreal objects," "values," "social orders," and "cultural entities," as well as "real objects," "existences," and "facts," and since not only "being" but also "nothingness" is fully "objective," phenomenology finds that there is a category more fundamental and more profound in experience than the category of "being" or "reality." It is the category of "object" in general. As Berger puts it concisely:

> [The] phenomenological reduction is less the passage from the object to the subject than the realization of the world as object, as phenomenon—*qua cogitatum*. . . . there is a more profound category than that of being and nonbeing, that of the object as thought [p. 41].

And later:

> We do not lose being by being exclusively interested in meanings, because the field of meaning is more vast than that of being. To have a "sense" is not a certain manner of being. It is being, on the contrary, which is a certain meaning. It no longer appears as the general and absolute background against which everything stands out. It is a sense, an idea [p. 76].

Therefore, when Berger said that transcendental subjectivity does not "make" anything, he meant that it does not ever make anything "real." It does not add to reality anything other than a reference to its own intentional activity; it adds a coating of "intendedness" or "meantness" which, upon reflection, can be distinguished from the empirical things and events in the real world which carry these meanings (or "essences"); and this "meantness" can thus be entertained just as such, just as *cogitata*, without our taking into account the always presupposed reference these *cogitata* may carry within themselves to the real things and events they are the meanings *of*. In short, the transcendental reduction, i.e., the reduction to the pure having-of-objects by the mind, is the final and absolutely correct manner of making the distinction between meaning and reference.

UP TO NOW we have not said anything particularly new or starᵗˡⁱng for Husserl scholarship, though we may be disposed to admire the typically Latin lucidity with which the French mind deals with the Germanic obscurities found in Husserl's own texts and vocabulary. It is rather in the peculiar manner in which Berger develops the theory of transcendental consciousness that we detect his special accent. We must remember that Berger belonged to what is now called the School of Aix-en-Provence [9] and which consisted, apart from himself, of his predecessors, Blondel, Segond, and Paliard, as well as his lifelong friend and inspiration, René Le Senne. It was the affinities he discovered between the thought of Le Senne and Husserl that inspired his first extensive reading of German philosophy and his desire to make it better known in France. Behind Blondel and Le Senne stood, naturally, Descartes, the tradition of "reflexive analysis," and Kant. Brunschvicg and Hamelin are, after these, among the authors most frequently quoted.

Provence, and the south of France generally, is considerably more "Latin," or perhaps one should say more "Mediterranean," than Paris. Its concerns are considerably more practical, more ethical, more "spiritualistic" than those of Paris. When Berger speaks of the transcendental ego as a "nothingness," [10] this is much less in the sense of Sartre or William James than in the sense of Saint Teresa of Avila and John of the Cross. He was

9. See Roger Mucchielli, *op. cit.*, p. 364.

10. Gaston Berger, "Caractère et liberté," *Les Etudes philosophiques.* XIV (1959), 50.

greatly interested in Oriental philosophy and "mysticism" (a word we must always keep in quotation marks because of his otherwise thoroughgoing rationalism); there is more that binds him to the African philosophers, Saint Augustine and Albert Camus, than he fully admitted or even, perhaps, consciously realized.

Despite his frequent rejections of *existential* interpretations of Husserl and in spite of his frequent reminders that Husserl's philosophy is based on an analysis of "the idea of science," that it is not "mystical" (p. 33), but that it rather results in ideal, atemporal demonstrations which must have the character of "rigorous science" (p. 50), Berger nevertheless cannot help going straight to those few passages in Husserl in which he speaks of the "higher" problems of history, culture, ethics, and religion, "of death, of fate, of the possibility of a 'genuine' human life." [11] "Phenomenology," Berger writes, "does not seek self-experience but self-understanding" (p. 74). In its completed form it must consist of a coherent system of propositions "built progressively, on indubitable foundations," and capable of "forcing itself on every rational being" (p. 27). Yet, in its progressive "intentional analysis" of the sense of the experienced world, phenomenology can and does pose even the questions of death and of the absurd (pp. 82 ff.), insofar as it seeks to "find the sense" of these "existential" phenomena. For Berger, the understanding of death is not a *cosmological* but an *ontological* (i.e., in Husserl's sense, *conceptual*) question. "It is not a question of lasting, but of being. . . . I have nothing to hope for from the simple prolongation of my life." [12] Through the transcendental reduction existence can be clarified in its "ontological" as opposed to its merely factual or empirical sense. In a poignant passage that reminds one of Heidegger (though he disliked Heidegger's interpretation of phenomenology), Berger writes:

Having been born into the world without reason or for some reason which we cannot understand, committed to a fate which we are unable to fathom, we come to ourselves in reflection only to find

11. Edmund Husserl, *Cartesian Meditations*, p. 156, quoted by Berger on p. 90.
12. Gaston Berger, "Caractère et liberté," pp. 50–51.

that the act of grasping ourselves in false images of ourselves throws us ahead of ourselves. Held between a world in which we cannot have complete confidence and an absolute which we never attain, we are, as philosophers, plunged into the same dark night of the soul which the mystics speak of.[13]

Two things are to be noted here, in conclusion. The first is very simple, and straightforwardly Husserlian: the transcendental reduction is a turn away from real, existential, factual things and events to their meanings. When Husserl poses the question of "the origin of the world," it is not to ask, like the Pre-Socratic Greek cosmologists, where it came from or what it is made of, but rather: What does it "mean"? What is the "sense" of the world as the organized totality of objects within which all human experience must, by definition, take place? Similarly, Berger, even in posing the "higher" philosophical problems, approaches them in a nonpsychologistic and nonempirical manner, not to tell stories or make empirical generalizations on the basis of case histories, but to examine the higher and more exalted manifestations of the human spirit in their eidetic "sense."

But there is something else, something which is not fully accounted for simply by saying that Berger was unable, in spite of himself, to fully stifle his "Mediterranean" preoccupation with death, fate, destiny, and practical philosophy. His friends thought of him as another Marcus Aurelius; he thought of himself as a Montaigne.[14] It was the *second* step of transcendental phenomenology in which he was most interested: having discovered the world as a system of "constituted objects," it is the constituting consciousness itself which most interests Berger. We must *begin* with the "constituted sense," but we must ultimately account for this sense in terms of intentional acts of transcendental subjectivity. Berger's interpretation of Husserl here is very sure, but it is also quite free—in the hands of one who has the full confidence of a complete illumination, of having grasped the mind of the master wholly and completely.

Berger emphasizes the difficulty of Husserl's thought on this matter: it does not offer us "easy access" (p. 39); to understand

13. As quoted by Roger Mucchielli, *op. cit.*, p. 372.
14. Joseph Moreau, "Sagesse de Gaston Berger," *Les Etudes philosophiques*, XVI (1961), 340.

the transcendental reduction "is far from an easy thing." There are even "moral conditions," principally an "uncommon detachment" (p. 42), required for grasping the transcendental ego; it must be pursued "over a long period of time"; and, when it is finally revealed, it appears more as a "gratuitous event" than anything we have accomplished deliberately (p. 43). He does not hesitate to speak of learning to practice the transcendental method as a kind of "conversion" (pp. 44, 51), which releases a new "intellectual dynamic" (p. 46):

> . . . we could say that the phenomenological reduction "presupposes itself." This is basically the scandal of every conversion: it seems necessary, afterwards, to those who have been converted, but it seems paradoxical to those who have not yet surrendered themselves. This is because the phenomenological reduction is not a possibility of man; it is a possibility of the transcendental ego we truly are without knowing it [pp. 44–45].

My natural being as a man, as a character, a personality, an "empirical ego," is wholly in the world; it constitutes one of the several realms of objectivity in which we lead our natural lives. But underlying the very possibility of objectifying ourselves and our lives is our *virtual* but never fully explicit awareness of the impersonal, nonegological,[15] i.e., transcendental, subjectivity which is the condition of any objectivity whatsoever, including our own self-objectifications. This transcendental ego, which we most truly are without knowing it, is "extraworldly" and "in some sense ineffable" (p. 49) because it can never be brought to full reflexive clarity, it can never be *objectified*. Berger speaks frequently and eloquently of the ascetic attitude of detachment necessary to practice the *epochē* ("suspension of judgment" concerning the world, things in the world, even our own feelings, emotions, and inner psychological life). Such an act of detachment does not alter anything either within or outside us; it only enables us to take both the world and ourselves as beings in the world in their objectively constituted sense. "For the phenomenologist," writes Berger, "psychological consciousness, man's soul, is in the 'world' " (p. 35).

15. Gaston Berger, *Recherches sur les conditions de la connaissance: Essai d'une théorétique pure* (Paris: Presses Universitaires de France, 1941), pp. 96 ff. Cf. Henry Duméry, *op. cit.*, p. 356.

The discovery of transcendental subjectivity is something completely unique. On the one hand, as Husserl says in *Ideas*, every ego (i.e., "every stream of experience") is capable of grasping its own indubitable and absolute existence with the self-evidence of immediate insight:

> I apprehend an absolute Self whose existence is, in principle, undeniable, that is, the insight that it does not exist is, in principle, impossible; it would be nonsense to maintain the possibility of an experience given in such a way not truly existing. The stream of experience which is mine, that, namely, of the one who is thinking, may be to ever so great an extent uncomprehended, unknown in its past and future reaches, yet as soon as I glance towards the flowing life and into the real present it flows through, and in so doing grasp myself as the pure subject of this life . . . I say forthwith and because I must: *I am,* this life is, I live: *cogito*.[16]

Moreover, what I grasp is not only that there is a stream of experience taking place here but that this consciousness is the absolute theater of being for me. This consciousness is coextensive with the whole of being in such wise that I can "doubt" all other things, events, all other consciousnesses, but I cannot doubt that it *seems* to me that I perceive these things, events, persons, etc. It is the world which is "contingent" and consciousness which is "necessary":

> The world is not doubtful in the sense that there are rational grounds which might be pitted against the tremendous force of unanimous experiences, but in the sense that a doubt is *thinkable,* and this is so because the possibility of non-being is in principle never excluded.[17]

It is an essential feature of the "thing-world" that its existence is never *necessarily* guaranteed by its givenness to consciousness; whereas it is an essential feature of consciousness that it is the *necessary* condition of the givenness or appearance of anything whatsoever.

Thus far Descartes was correct. But Husserl goes on to observe that this *necessity* within my own experience is an "ontic"

16. Edmund Husserl, *Ideas*, trans. W. R. Boyce-Gibson (London: Allen & Unwin, 1931), § 46, p. 143.
17. *Ibid.*, p. 145.

or "empirical" necessity; it is a *Faktum*, an existential intuition which is valid only once, i.e., only for me, and not for everyone or from all perspectives.[18] Therefore, this *existential necessity* must be completed by becoming the object of an intentional analysis. Its conceptual features are disclosed through a method of eidetic intuition which takes this existential fact (of the indubitable givenness of the world to my consciousness) *as an example* of consciousness as such. By freely varying this example in imagination, I can discover its eidetically necessary structures and, in that way, will add an eidetic necessity to an empirical necessity. Since every individual instance of an essential type must exemplify the essential structures and characteristics of that type, we need no more than one example—and in any case we can never have, in this instance, more than one example— namely, our own ego-life. Through eidetic analysis we are able to ascend from the example to the type, to transcend the factual reality of our own individual, "solipsistic" consciousness to discover in eidetic intuition what is necessary and true for *any* consciousness. The existential intuition is valid only for me; the eidetic intuition is true for all.

Thus far Husserl. Now, if we turn to Berger's analysis, we will find, I think, that he is less interested in the eidetic and conceptual unfolding of the essential structures of consciousness —though he in no way neglects this and in fact shows in several instances how Husserl solves problems by an eidetic investigation of the *sense* of "thing," "other person," etc.—than in the question of the ultimate transcendental *fact* of consciousness. If there are sometimes exaggerations in his terminology, they all come from this absorption in what Husserl also termed the "miraculous fact" *that consciousness is.*

Berger approaches the problem as follows:

Realism is . . . correct in affirming the transcendence of real things in relation to consciousness, since it also places itself in the natural attitude, which opposes the soul to its body and to bodies. In the vast cosmos man is only a miserably limited being, and one must agree that it is laughable to reduce the being of the entire world to nothing but a human dream—as subjective idealism

18. *Ibid.*

would attempt to do—since man in turn is only a fragment of the world. The philosopher finds himself caught in a vicious circle if he does not raise himself to the level of transcendental subjectivity [p. 36].

We must learn to distinguish the transcendental from the psychological; we must push beyond any introspection into our own psychological states, since these, too, are "objects" of consciousness. It is precisely the consciousness which grasps itself as an object but is itself never truly "grasped" which is our goal. Eidetic questions are not, it is true, empirical but conceptual questions (p. 57), and phenomenology is an eidetic investigation. Yet we must acknowledge that we can elaborate a valid concept of the *eidos ego* only by performing the transcendental reduction, i.e., by discovering those perfectly typical and eidetically universalizable *acts of consciousness as such* which make the appearance of the world, as well as of myself experiencing the world, possible. This is the discovery not only of a *transcendental law* but of its correlative, *transcendental fact,* as well. A psychological reduction would not be sufficient; we cannot elaborate a valid concept of the *eidos ego* on the basis of the empirical psychological ego, because this ego is just another "worldly" thing. The *transcendental ego,* however, cannot be resolved into either fact or essence for the reason that "the *cogito* founds both fact and essence" (p. 60); it is the "extrawordly condition of all meaning" (p. 62).

"The *transcendental,*" writes Berger,

> is not set against the *world* as two regions which would be distinguished at the center of being: it has a manner of being proper to itself. . . . It does not claim to reveal to us *another* world. . . . The ego's life transcends the world, not because it is foreign to the world, but because it *constitutes* the world [p. 72].

This is clearly an *interpretation* of Husserl (which goes beyond the division of ontology into the "region" of the world and the "region" of consciousness as this is presented in the *Ideas*), but it is a perfectly coherent and disciplined interpretation. Berger stresses the transcendentalism of the *Cartesian Meditations* and in so doing gives Husserl's transcendental idealism (a term which does not occur in the *Ideas*) a new focus and provides it with a new ambition. The reason why the phenomenological attitude is "always difficult to effect" (p. 55) and requires such uncommon detachment from the world is that transcendental consciousness itself always escapes our grasp; it is always ahead of any particular reflection, as the unfathomable condition of all experience and reflection; it is impersonal and absolute. Berger seems to feel that Husserl may have been overly optimistic when he claimed that he could elaborate a "science" of the transcendental ego. All we can ever know "scientifically" (i.e., eidetically), he seems to say, are its effects. All knowledge is the result of reflection, and, in this sense, we cannot "know" the transcendental ego. But, if we cannot fully "know" it, we can, says Berger, "live" it ever more fully; his philosophy is not only a new way of knowing but also a new way of living.

As we pointed out at the outset, Gaston Berger's central interest in phenomenology was the theory of constitution; his originality was to give an interpretation of transcendental constituting consciousness which is as much ethical as it is epistemological.

JAMES M. EDIE

Northwestern University
December 19, 1971

Translator's Note

IN ADDITION to the standard problems involved in translating a philosophical text, the present work raises a number of interesting historical problems. Written over thirty years ago, at a time when Husserl's work was still generally unknown in France, Berger intended his book to be an introduction to phenomenology, which would situate certain phenomenological advances in line with traditional French philosophy. As an introductory work, *The* Cogito *in Husserl's Philosophy* had few French sources to draw upon, no established phenomenological vocabulary, and, except for the use of the French translation of the *Cartesian Meditations*, all passages taken from Husserl's works were translated by Berger himself.

Since that time, of course, new editions of Husserl's texts have appeared and numerous translations are to be found in French and in English. The passages cited by Berger have been checked against the current German texts and against existing translations, and have been altered when necessary. In addition, references to the *Krisis* as it appeared in the periodical, *Philosophia* (Belgrade, 1936), have been transposed to include the corresponding references in the current *Husserliana* edition (The Hague, 1954) and in the English translation (Evanston, 1970). Berger's references to the 1913 edition of *Ideen* have been retained, as they are indicated in the present *Husserliana* edition (The Hague, 1950).

In dealing with quotes from the *Cartesian Meditations* other

problems have arisen. Berger relies upon the 1931 French translation, and, although both a German and an English edition have
since been published, each is based on different manuscripts. The
series of lectures delivered at the Sorbonne in 1929 were revised
by Husserl for the French translation and then continued to be
reworked by him until his death. The 1950 *Husserliana* edition
includes these revisions, and the 1960 English translation is
based on both the French and German editions and also includes
the original text of 1929. We find, then, that, unlike the other
works, where one is dealing with translations of a given German
text, each edition of the *Cartesian Meditations* is in some sense a
distinct work. So, whenever—and this holds for the majority of
the cases—the texts do correspond, the English edition has been
cited; in those cases where the passages differ, the French text
used by Berger is given and the reference to the corresponding
passage in the English edition is also indicated.

Another research problem involves Berger's repeated reference to certain unpublished manuscripts in which Husserl deals
with questions of constitution. Because his references to these
writings are of an extremely general nature, it has been impossible to pinpoint particular manuscripts. Since the publication of
The Cogito *in Husserl's Philosophy*, however, works have appeared which develop the theory of constitution: *Ideen* II and III
(1952) and *Analysen zur passiven Synthesis* (1966). The Husserl Archives also contain numerous manuscripts on constitution,
under the following classifications:

C. Zeitkonstitution als formale Konstitution
D. Primordiale Konstitution ("Urkonstitution")
E. Intersubjektive Konstitution

The work involved in tracking down references to early editions, to transcribed but unpublished manuscripts, and to bibliographical works now out of print was made so much easier and
more enjoyable through the facilities of the Husserl Archives at
the Sorbonne, kindly provided by Paul Ricoeur. Most especially,
I would like to thank Dorian Tiffeneau for her invaluable help in
researching the texts available in the Archives. I am deeply in-
debted to Marjorie Grene for her help throughout the translation,
for guidance in questions of phenomenological terminology and

German vocabulary, and for suggestions concerning questions of style and readability. I would also like to thank Virginia Seidman for her thorough editing of the translation. To my husband, Michael, for his encouragement, suggestions, and assistance in typing the manuscript, my fondest thanks.

KATHLEEN McLAUGHLIN

Paris
December, 1971

The *Cogito* in
Husserl's Philosophy

To J. Segond,
    as a respectful token of gratitude

1 / The Central Position of the *Cogito*

IN THESE PAGES we intend to study a topic that is at the very center of the philosophy of Edmund Husserl: the realization of the "I think," the recognition of transcendental subjectivity, the *cogito*.

For Husserl, the *cogito* does not appear fully elucidated from the beginning of the investigation. In order to understand its meaning and to see all its importance, it is necessary to make a preliminary effort, to accomplish an ordered series of intellectual steps, and even to effect "a radical conversion of our entire existence." [1]

This attitude might surprise a French reader. Steeped in Descartes, we "depart" willingly with him from the *cogito* to build, on the solid foundation of what seems an indisputable experience, the varied edifices of our particular philosophies. French thought is prospective. German thought is, on the contrary, attracted more by the profound than by the prolific. Instead of expanding, it burrows. German thought wants to justify its affirmations or its flights either by a series, often minutely detailed, of abstract reasonings or by a concrete approach to the hidden being which is at the origin of things.

On this score Husserl's originality is thus not so much that he searched over a long period for an absolute principle and an as-

1. Eugen Fink, "Was will die Phänomenologie Edmund Husserls?," *Die Tatwelt*, X, No. 1 (Berlin, 1934), 15. (This article will henceforth be cited as "E. Fink, 'Was will. . . .'")

sured foundation for his philosophy, as it is that he wanted to justify in this way what seems to us by its nature to need no justification: the "I think." What could be more certain, but also what could be simpler, than this affirmation? One admits without difficulty that one can start from the *cogito;* it is not so easy to see how one could arrive at it.

Justifying the *cogito* seems to us a less paradoxical undertaking, however, if we notice how easily it is wrongly understood and given differing interpretations. The more we believe it to be a self-evident affirmation, the more its meaning escapes us. For Descartes himself, so direct and so disdainful of vain subtleties, the *cogito* is not a cognition unsupported by anything else. It is preceded by methodological doubt, that is, by a critical examination, by a preliminary reflection. Sometimes one passes too quickly over the first two *Meditations,* drawn as one is by the divine perfection to be discovered or by the physical world to be reconstructed. Yet it is from these first two *Meditations* that Husserl will be inspired in his *Cartesian Meditations* by trying to protect himself more successfully from haste and from bias than had the author of the *Discourse on Method.* Phenomenology could thus almost be called "a neo-Cartesianism, even though it is obliged—and precisely by its radical development of Cartesian motifs—to reject nearly all the well-known doctrinal content of the Cartesian philosophy." [2]

The importance attached to the *cogito* does not characterize Husserl's "point of view"; he has repeatedly denied that he is producing "a point-of-view philosophy," which would always rest on certain prejudices. He wants "to start from what is found before all points of view, from the whole of what offers itself to intuition before any thought constructive of theories, from all that one can see and grasp directly when one does not allow oneself to be blinded by prejudices or to be diverted by these prejudices from taking into consideration the complete series of true givens." [3] One must not imagine Husserl accepting the *cogito* be-

2. Edmund Husserl, *Cartesian Meditations,* trans. Dorion Cairns (The Hague: Martinus Nijhoff, 1960), p. 1. (Henceforth cited as "*CM.*") [With a few exceptions, noted as they occur, page references throughout are to the Cairns translation.—Translator.]

3. Edmund Husserl, *Ideen zu einer reinen Phänomenologie und phäno-*

forehand and searching outside for its logical supports and rational props. It is by following the normal course of his reflections that he succeeds in grasping the original nature of the "I think." A concrete thought does not start with the *cogito;* it starts with things, with confused experience which is not yet very clearly either this or that. It conquers the *cogito* in the progressive elucidation of the difficulties to which it applies itself.

This means that our effort to expose the preparation of the *cogito* will have to retrace in some sense the history of Husserl's thought. But we will be concerned with the analyses carried out in Husserl's early works only to the extent that they prepare the way for the discovery of the *cogito.* Moreover, if it is true, as Husserl maintains and as we ourselves believe, that the *cogito* is the essential moment of phenomenology, then a historical study, directed in the spirit we are suggesting, should allow us to separate the essential from the accessory and to place again in their true perspective, as elements of a general program, what some have taken for definitive and self-sufficient results.

Thus we tend to apply to Husserl's thought the method he himself proposes to us to use for the history of philosophy in general, that is, a "historico-teleological" [4] reflection, a study which does not originate from outside, by considering a thought

menologischen Philosophie, 3d ed. (Halle, 1928), p. 38. The first edition dates from 1913. (Henceforth cited as *"Ideen."*) [Only *Ideen I* had been published when Berger wrote *The* Cogito *in Husserl's Philosophy.*—Translator.]

4. Edmund Husserl, "Die Krisis der europäischen Wissenschaften und die transzendentale Phänomenologie," *Philosophia,* I (Belgrade, 1936), 77; *Krisis,* p. XIV, n. 3; *Crisis,* p. 3, n. 1. (Henceforth cited as " 'Krisis,' " "Krisis," and "*Crisis.*" See below.)

[The only "Krisis" text to which Berger had access was that published in the journal *Philosophia.* Since this may not be readily available, I have provided cross-references to the *Husserliana* volume and to the recent translation by David Carr, based on it: *Die Krisis der europäischen Wissenschaften und die transzendentale Phänomenologie: Eine Einleitung in die phänomenologische Philosophie,* Husserliana, Vol. VI (The Hague: Martinus Nijhoff, 1954; second printing, 1962), ed. Walter Biemel; and *The Crisis of European Sciences and Transcendental Phenomenology: An Introduction to Phenomenological Philosophy,* trans. David Carr (Evanston: Northwestern University Press, 1970). All footnote references to the *Krisis* will thus appear in triple form as "Krisis" (*Philosophia*), *Krisis* (*Husserliana*), and *Crisis* (Carr translation).—Translator.]

as a succession of events, but which insists in finding it from within, in order to arrive at the "critical comprehension of the total unity of history." [5] The sense of a philosophical thought resides, then, in the *intention* which subtends its successive manifestations and not in the particular affirmations that it has been led to make; it is too easy to interpret these affirmations as one pleases when they are artificially detached from the living movement of which they are only elements without autonomy of their own.

Moreover, this first historical approach may present some interest for the French reader to whom phenomenology is still not well known because of a lack of translations. This is true despite some fine general studies, which, however, preceded Husserl's later works, which are particularly important for the subject that concerns us.

The historical approach also provides us with the opportunity to emphasize the profound unity of Husserlian thought and the continuity of its development. The astonishment with which the philosophical world greeted Husserl's *Ideen,* and then his *Logic* and his *Cartesian Meditations,* is perhaps due to the Cartesian idea—or at least the idea attributed to Descartes—of the immediate and simple nature of the *cogito.* The *cogito* seems so naturally a point of departure, it appears so emphatically to be able to be only what it is, that, seeing it introduced into the very center of Husserlian reflection, one had the feeling of a new beginning on new foundations. No one dreamed of seeing in it the natural outcome of previous work; and the legend was created of a Husserl who had been a realist and was then supposed to have suddenly denied his former assertions in his conversion to idealism.[6]

This thesis of Husserl's "two philosophies" could be maintained only if the philosopher's intention had been modified in the course of his research. We believe we can establish that this is not so. Admittedly, there is a noticeable transformation in perspective, in affirmations, in vocabulary between the earlier writ-

5. "Krisis," p. 146; *Krisis,* p. 72; *Crisis,* p. 71.
6. Examples of this interpretation can be found in the discussion which developed at Juvisy on September 12, 1932, in the course of a symposium dedicated to phenomenology by the Société thomiste (*Journées d'études de la Société thomiste,* I [Juvisy: Editions du Cerf, 1932]).

ings and the later works. But it takes place in the course of the progressive deepening of an investigation which does not wander from its axis. The *Ideen* is new in comparison to the *Logische Untersuchungen*, which itself goes far beyond the *Philosophie der Arithmetik.* Here, however, it is only a question of the normal progress of a thought which is not idling in place.

If we were dealing with a philosophy of synthesis, we could speak of deviation, or at least of new philosophical thought, in connection with any construction which would bring about the intervention of adventitious elements differing profoundly from those one originally admitted and proceeding from which one felt able to resolve the problems one had posed. Such a judgment would not be applicable to Husserl, who has always denied making constructions and who displays a profound aversion to any "system." He does not want to erect his own in the face of those already existing or even to base his own concepts on "the critique of any system, whether contemporary or coming to us from antiquity." [7] He wants "to guide, not to instruct, but only to indicate; [he is] trying to describe what [he] see[s]." [8]

In the course of an investigation undertaken in this spirit, it is natural that the concepts used in the beginning be gradually modified as the analysis progresses and as new implications appear. Instead of a rigorous fidelity to initial definitions, here there must be great docility toward the subject matter being studied. This is the primary meaning that must be given to the principle of the return to the things themselves, *"zu den Sachen selbst,"* where some have wanted to see a realist manifesto:

> To pass judgment on things in a reasonable or a scientific manner is to direct oneself *toward the things themselves,* that is, to return from words and opinions back to the things themselves, to question their self-givenness and to leave aside all prejudices irrelevant to the thing.[9]

At the beginning of an investigation, overly precise definitions are not without danger:

7. "Krisis," p. 146; *Krisis,* p. 72; *Crisis,* p. 71.
8. "Krisis," p. 95; *Krisis,* p. 17; *Crisis,* p. 18.
9. *Ideen,* p. 35.

It must be remarked, moreover, in a completely general sense, that at the beginning of phenomenology all concepts, all terms, must remain as it were, in a state of becoming, always ready to be differentiated in conformity with the progress of the analysis of consciousness and of the knowledge of new phenomenological levels inside of what at first appeared an undivided unity.[10]

Alongside this submission to the real, there must be found in the phenomenologist a persevering demand for lucidity which can tirelessly carry out the "patient investigations of detail" which Husserl foresaw as early as 1891, when he sought "stable foundations." [11]

If phenomenology has oriented itself toward transcendental investigations, it is because, in "its effort toward a radical logic," [12] it has recognized that, to establish itself solidly, logic must "return in a systematic manner from ideal forms," which it might at first be tempted to consider as its unique domain, "to consciousness, which constitutes them phenomenologically." [13] "Can one avoid these transcendental problems when one wants to understand logic . . . , where one wants, not to *speculate* on being and on the theory of being, but to let oneself be led by the degrees and the depths of meaning? He who says A here, must also say B." [14]

These, then, are the successive implications that Husserl seeks to discover. Conceived in this spirit,

the investigations have a quality of relativity, troublesome, yet inevitable; they are provisional and not definitive, as one would have wished, and this is because, on the level where it has placed itself, each investigation triumphs over some naïveté yet still carries with it the naïveté inherent in this level, which in turn will have to be surpassed by more penetrating investigations.[15]

10. *Ibid.*, p. 170.
11. Edmund Husserl, *Philosophie der Arithmetik: I. Psychologische und logische Untersuchungen* (Halle: Pfeffer, 1891), p. V. (Henceforth cited as *"Arithmetik."*)
12. Edmund Husserl, *Formale und transzendentale Logik* (Halle: Niemeyer, 1929), p. 228. (Henceforth cited as *"Logik."*)
13. *Ibid.*, p. 233.
14. *Ibid.*, pp. 238–39.
15. *Ibid.*, p. 239.

It is a question, therefore, of seeing more and more clearly, more and more profoundly, and of describing faithfully. Without destroying what has already been established, the analysis, as it proceeds, gives it a new and more exact interpretation. Again, it is not a question here of "real" analyses, in the usual sense of the term, but of "intentional" analyses, that is to say, analyses which aim at "uncovering intentional implications." [16]

The tenacious idea of Husserl's dual philosophy has for its origin also the existence of disciples more concerned with developing their personal philosophies, that is, with *using* Husserl, than with translating the profound inspiration of the master and remaining faithful to it. If there is duality of inspiration, this was established between Husserl and those who call themselves phenomenologists without committing themselves to following him; it is not in the thought of the founder of phenomenology. The only unity that can rightfully be demanded of his works is an intentional unity, and this appears manifest to us. We hope to demonstrate it in the first part of this work, which will lead us to the *cogito* in a natural and, it seems to us, a necessary manner.

We will next have to examine the *cogito* itself from a double point of view: on the one hand, by elucidating the characteristic features of the original step which introduces it (the phenomenological reduction); on the other, by inquiring what meaning of the ego it is at which one thus arrives. We will then show how the *cogito*, if it is the goal of a difficult and prolonged preliminary reflection, is also the point of departure of later analyses, which Husserl terms "constitutive." The two essential themes of phenomenology are the theory of reduction and the theory of constitution. [17] Now, the reduction is the preparation of the *cogito*, and the constitutive investigations are its explicitation. So it is with good reason that we make the *cogito* the central problem of phenomenology. It is within it that the phenomenological conversion takes place, "the reversal of the fundamental and permanent attitude of human life" [18] by which we are introduced into a

---

16. *Ibid.*, p. 185. See also p. 217.

17. Eugen Fink, "Die phänomenologische Philosophie Edmund Husserls in der gegenwärtigen Kritik," *Kantstudien*, XXXVIII, Nos. 3–4 (1933), 344. (Henceforth cited as "E. Fink, 'Die phänom.'")

18. E. Fink, "Was will . . . ," p. 16.

new "dimension," that of the transcendental, "long foreseen and yet still hidden." [19]

For the reasons briefly indicated above, it will be seen that we have not been concerned with those who have more or less submitted to Husserl's influence and who are called, vaguely and rather inexactly, phenomenologists. What has contributed most to distorting the ideas that have been formed concerning Husserlian thought—and this in Germany even more than in France —is the desire to interpret it in terms of those disciples who were held to be orthodox. If these phenomenologists can be understood only through Husserl, it is impossible, on the contrary, to understand Husserl if he is seen through Scheler or Heidegger.

19. "Krisis," p. 175; *Krisis,* p. 104; *Crisis,* p. 100.

2 / The Preparation of Transcendental Phenomenology

THE FIRST PHILOSOPHICAL WORK of Edmund Husserl was the *Philosophy of Arithmetic*, published in 1891. Here the author intended to "prepare by a series of psychological and logical investigations the scientific foundations upon which one could later establish mathematics and philosophy." [1] Thus at the outset there appeared what was to be Husserl's constant preoccupation: the desire for a perfect justification—arithmetic and philosophy must be *founded*. The *Logic* of 1929 claims to do nothing else; here, the problem only widens to include the natural sciences as well as arithmetic. The word "foundation" returns repeatedly in the work of 1891, notably in the passage—quoted above [2]—where Husserl intends to reach it by "patient analyses of detail." [3] It will also be found in one of the last books he published: "Our general aim, which is to give an absolute foundation to the sciences. . . ." [4]

1. Edmund Husserl, *Arithmetik*, p .V.
2. *Supra*, p. 8.
3. *Arithmetik*, p. V.
4. Edmund Husserl, *Méditations cartésiennes: Introduction à la Phénoménologie*, trans. Gabrielle Peiffer and Emmanuel Levinas (Paris, 1931), p. 7. [Dorion Cairns's English translation of this same passage reads: "The general aim of grounding science absolutely . . ." (p. 8). Because of Berger's emphasis on the word *foundation*, I have used the French translation here, but both are acceptable renderings of the German: "das allgemeine Ziel absoluter Wissenschaftsbegründung . . ." (Edmund Husserl, *Cartesianische Meditationen und Pariser Vorträge* [The Hague: Martinus Nijhoff, 1950], p. 49).—TRANSLATOR.]

In the *Philosophy of Arithmetic* we see already at work the method of "intentional analysis," constantly employed by Husserl, a method which leads to clarifying what is implied in the meaning of perceptions experienced or of concepts studied. For example, by analyzing the idea of number, one understands that it implies the idea of multiplicity.[5]

Of what does this implication consist? Sometimes simply— and that is the case here—in the fact of presupposing some other simpler notion indispensable to the understanding of the one in question. But the relations which clarify one another in this way remain purely ideal. For Husserl it is always understanding that is in question and not in any way sensing. Nothing is farther from phenomenology than a philosophy of internal experience.

The implication is not always so simple, and we will have the opportunity to demonstrate this in studying the "phenomenological reduction." It does not consist solely in reaching the genus in the species. It also leads to transcending the given in order to complete it by all that it lacks *actually* but which must nevertheless be restored to it so that its meaning may appear.

The *Cartesian Meditations* will specify the precise difference that separates intentional analysis from an ordinary analysis, in the common sense of the term. The latter separates a whole into its elements. To be sure, intentional analysis sometimes carries out explicitations of this kind, "but everywhere its peculiar attainment (as 'intentional') is an uncovering of the *potentialities* 'implicit' in actualities of consciousness."[6] It thus tends to make explicit "what is consciously meant" (*ibid.*).

Let us limit ourselves now to pointing out this demand for transcendence inherent in phenomenology from its beginnings, which accounts for its fecundity as well as for its evolution. Arithmetic poses the problem of logic, of which it is only a specification; it requires that the nature of this pure logic be made precise, the "theoretical science, independent of any psychology and of any empirical investigation, which includes within its natural limits all pure arithmetic and the entire theory of multiplic-

5. *Arithmetik*, Chap. I, § 1, pp. 8 ff.
6. Edmund Husserl, *CM*, p. 46.

ity." [7] Logic, in turn, has meaning only in terms of ideal essences, beyond the purely natural given; it supposes that significations transcend signs. But this relation of the sign to the signification is finally comprehensible only as the function of a transcendental subject. The ultimate term of our implications is the "I."

In connection with the mathematical questions to which his interest was directed in 1891, Husserl was already thinking about looking for justification on the side of the subject: "Numbers," he wrote, "are constituted by the act of counting multiplicities." [8] But he had not yet made the distinction between the soul and the "I," between psychology and transcendental phenomenology, and it is from psychology that he awaits the solution to the problems which preoccupy him. Thirty-eight years later the *Logic* will employ an analogous formula: "To count is to produce numbers." [9] But it will be able to show that the meaning of this sentence can be completely elucidated only by referring back to an intentional subjectivity "in which the products which are effected and which have been effected are constituted as synthetic unities." [10]

In the years immediately following the publication of the *Philosophy of Arithmetic,* Husserl believes that descriptive and genetic psychology will be able to remove all the difficulties of logic and of the theory of knowledge. In particular, he wrote in 1894, "I believe I can claim that no theory of judgment will be capable of agreeing with the facts if it does not rest on a thorough study of the descriptive and genetic relations of intuitions and representations." [11]

And it is still from a descriptive and genetic study that the most recent phenomenology hopes to receive all the clarity we are capable of obtaining in these matters, but the investigation will take on an entirely new significance, since it will be carried out in the transcendental dimension, after the conversion realized by the phenomenological reduction. By way of these exam-

7. Edmund Husserl, "Selbstanzeige der Logischen Untersuchungen," *Vierteljahrsschrift für wissenschaftliche Philosophie,* XXIV (1900), 511.
8. *Arithmetik,* p. 202.
9. Edmund Husserl, *Logik,* p. 39.
10. Edmund Husserl, "Psychologische Studien zur elementaren Logik," *Philosophische Monatshefte,* XXX (1894), 187.
11. *Ibid.*

ples, we see how little Husserl's preoccupations have varied since his first works but also how the progress of his reflection has given an original meaning to old problems and a precise formulation to anticipated solutions.

The elucidation that Husserl was seeking was, however, more difficult than he first believed. Only the first volume of the *Philosophy of Arithmetic* came out in 1891. The second never saw the light of day.

> Abandoned along the way by logic wherever I hoped to receive from it the solutions to precise questions I had to ask it, I was finally obliged to leave aside completely my investigations of mathematical philosophy until I should be able to arrive successfully at certain clarity in the essential questions of the theory of knowledge and in the critical comprehension of logic as science.[12]

It is only in 1929, in the *Logic*, that the problems of the foundation of the sciences in general and of mathematics in particular will actually be elucidated.[13] After the *Philosophy of Arithmetic*, Husserl finds himself forced to enlarge considerably the field of his investigations. The logic that he finds in his contemporaries, in Mill, in Spencer, in Sigwart, even in some neo-Kantians like Lange, is grounded in psychology. From then on, logic did not seem to him capable of giving an account of the necessity of the laws of thought and, in particular, of the rules of mathematics. How, in fact, "can the objectivity of mathematics and more generally of any science correspond to a psychological foundation of the logical?"[14] The Kantian solution does not seem to have held Husserl's attention in any profound way. He feels quite far from its complicated constructions. While he wants to go "to the things themselves," he sees the neo-Kantians of the Marburg school as substituting reflection on scientific theories for the direct study of known objects. Finally, transcendental reflection (in the Kantian sense of the term) does not seem to him to be radically different from psychology: "Transcendental psychology is precisely also a psychology."[15]

12. Edmund Husserl, *Logische Untersuchungen*, 1st ed. (Halle: Niemeyer, 1900), Vol. I, Preface, p. VII. (Henceforth cited as "*Log. Unt.*")
13. *Logik*, pp. 161 ff.
14. *Log. Unt.* (1st ed.), Vol. I, Preface, p. VII.
15. *Ibid.*, p. 93, note 3.

It is well known, he writes in the same place, that Kant's

theory of knowledge tends, in certain aspects, to rise above this psychologism of the powers of the soul considered as sources of knowledge; indeed, it is even successful in this. But it is enough here that it also presents important elements that result in psychologism, something which naturally does not exclude a vigorous polemic against other ways of founding knowledge on psychology [*ibid.*].

Husserl himself will thus have to build the logical theory of which he feels the need. This will be the object of the *Logical Investigations* and particularly of its first volume, published in 1900, which has for subtitle *Prolegomena to Pure Logic*.[16] Here Husserl intends "to open the way to a new conception of logic and to a new manner of treating it." [17] "I departed," he writes in the Preface to the *Logical Investigations*, "from the conviction then prevailing, and according to which it would be from psychology that the logic of the deductive sciences, like logic in general, would have to await its philosophical enlightenment." [18] Psychological analyses thus played a large role in the *Philosophy of Arithmetic*. But if they seemed useful in order to understand, for instance, the origin of mathematical representations, they appeared unable, on the other hand, to account for the objective nature and the internal unity proper to the "contents of thought."

The essential aim of the *Logical Investigations* is to radically distinguish logic from psychology, to show that logical operations are in no way comparable to real acts and that logical principles may not in any sense be considered as laws bearing on facts. They are ideal laws, and if one wishes to preserve a precise meaning for the sciences and for logic, one must carefully separate the psychological act by which these laws are thought from their

16. The French public possesses a very precise analysis of it due to V. Delbos (*Revue de métaphysique et de morale*, XIX, No. 5 [1911], 685–98). Charles Serrus has also clearly presented the conflict of psychologism and logic in his presentation of January 26, 1928, before the Société d'études philosophiques du Sud-Est (*Les Etudes philosophiques*, II, No. 1 [May, 1928], 9–18).
17. "Selbstanz.," p. 511.
18. *Log. Unt.* (1st ed). I, VI.

ideal essence toward which the concrete thoughts of individuals "tend." [19]

Husserl wants special attention paid to the essential difference that exists between "the anthropologically subjective unity of knowledge and the ideally objective unity of knowledge." [20] This permits a real understanding of the true nature of logical principles:

> The principle of contradiction, we are taught, is a judgment about judgments. To the extent to which one understands by judgments mental experiences, acts of holding-as-true, believing, etc. . . . this conception can have no value. He who states the principle makes a judgment, but neither the principle, nor that about which the principle judges, is a judgment.[21]

The principle of contradiction is not a "law for acts of judgment, but a law for the *contents of judgments* . . . or, in other words, for the *ideal meanings* that we are in the habit of calling simply propositions." [22]

Logical operations have an incontestable objectivity. They are immediately evident, their results perfectly necessary. How could one hope, without paradox, to deduce them from psychological laws that are poorly understood, uncertain, and without any precision?

Any true science must have an absolute quality.[23] To be sure, sciences as they are actually realized attain this ideal very imperfectly. Yet this is what gives them their particular meaning. The constructions of human reason merit the name of science in the degree to which they tend toward this absolute end.

If we apply intentional analysis to the idea of science, or more generally to the idea of theory, we bring to light what that idea necessarily entails if it is to have meaning. We then find two groups of conditions, some on the side of the object, others on the side of the subject.

19. This is what is expressed by the term "intention," which frequently appears in Husserl's writings and which he borrows from Brentano.
20. *Log. Unt.* (1st ed.), I, 174, § 47.
21. *Ibid.*, p. 176.
22. *Ibid.*
23. The introduction to the *Logik* begins with similar considerations (pp. 1 ff.).

With regard to the first group, it must be noted that the theory is not envisaged here as a system of subjective cognitions, empirically attached one to another, but as "an objective unity of *truths,* that is, of *propositions,* joined together by the relation of principle to consequence." [24] The conditions to be fulfilled are those necessary to preserve a meaning "for the ideas of truth, of proposition, of object, of manner of being, of relation, etc. . . . which essentially constitute the concept of theoretical unity" (*ibid.*).

The idea of truth, in turn, has meaning only if truth is one and if truth is objective, that is, independent of particular opinions and of the perspective from which one sees it.

Let us suppose that intelligent beings do not exist, that they are excluded by the order of nature, that is, that they are impossible as *real* beings—or let us suppose that beings capable of knowing certain categories of truths do not exist—then these ideal possibilities will remain without the reality to fill them; apprehension, knowledge, the conscious grasp of truth (or of certain categories of truths) will then be realized never and nowhere. Yet in itself each truth remains what it is; it conserves its ideal being.[25]

Note the word "real" in this passage. Truth does not imply any real beings capable of grasping it, but the restriction seems to indicate that it perhaps supposes a being for which it has meaning, a subject which would simply be located beyond what we understand by real, that is, beyond the world. Certainly this is not yet the discovery of transcendental subjectivity; it is at least a presentiment of it. The subjective conditions of any theory in general are ideal "and have their roots in the form of subjectivity in general and in its relation to knowledge." [26] It is only after the phenomenological reduction that the "subject" will appear in its originary power and that we will be able to get a clear idea of the sense that must be given to its ideality.

Theory, as justification of certain cognitions, is itself a cognition. In conformity with the rigorous meaning of truth that it

24. *Log. Unt.* (1st ed.), I, 111, § 32.
25. *Ibid.,* pp. 129–30, § 39.
26. *Ibid.,* p. 111, § 32.

wants to attain and to express, it could never be content with claims to truth; it must justify itself.[27] But if knowledge is absolute, how could this justification come about if not by the direct apprehension of truth? Just as the perfection of logical operations and the necessity of ideal connections render illegitimate any attempts to derive them from poorly assured psychological operations, of little certainty and completely obscure, so too the absolute nature of truth renders insufficient to insure its adequacy the guarantees supplied by subjective actions alone. Our human precautions are undoubtedly helpful in practice. In theory, however, they are of no interest unless self-evidence is possible. One cannot construct the absolute; one can only receive it. The rigorous idea of science and also of philosophy that Husserl entertains [28] necessarily implies the intuitionism which also characterizes his philosophical position. Truth supposes an intelligence capable of truth. Absolute reason is the correlative of absolute truth.

But this absolute reason, is it our own? This is not required by the idea of theory itself nor by that of truth. We find in Husserl, from the *Logical Investigations* on, the sense of the difference that exists between ideal evidence and human evidence. It is the ideal conditions and not the human, psychological conditions of knowledge that interest him.[29]

Thus the self-evident is the ideal form of perfect knowledge because it alone can deliver over to us the truth itself. If the subject who judges (and who is already conceived of as different from natural man)

> were never and nowhere able to experience in himself and to grasp as such that distinction which constitutes the justification of the judgment, if in all his judgments he lacked the self-evidence which distinguishes them from blind prejudices and which gives him the luminous certitude, not only to hold-as-true, but to possess the truth itself—then there would be no question for him of a ra-

---

27. *Ibid.*, p. 110.

28. One of Husserl's articles published in the periodical *Logos* in 1910 is entitled "Philosophie als strenge Wissenschaft." [English translation, "Philosophy as Rigorous Science," in Quentin Lauer, *Edmund Husserl: Phenomenology and the Crisis of Philosophy* (New York: Harper & Row, 1965), pp. 69–147.]

29. *Log. Unt.* (1st ed.), I, 237 ff., § 65.

tional establishment and foundation of knowledge, there would be no reason to speak of either theory or science.[30]

His analysis of the idea of theory, his radical distinction between psychology and logic, permit Husserl to disentangle the precise idea of a pure logic and to indicate the tasks incumbent on him: to fix pure categories of meaning and pure objective categories; to establish the theory of theoretically possible forms, that is, the pure theory of multiplicities.

It does not belong to our intention to enter into a detailed analysis of these propositions, nor do we think it necessary here to review the reasoning, at once conceptual and historical, by which Husserl maintains, against the psychologism of Hume, of Mill, of Spencer, against the anthropologism of Sigwart and Erdmann, his conception of pure logic. We only want to exhibit Husserl's leading idea in action, the search for an absolute foundation of science and philosophy. It is because it renders the idea of science, in the absolute sense of the word, incomprehensible that psychologism cannot account for logic: all psychologism is, in the final analysis, a skeptical relativism.

The radical distinction between psychology and logic, between established facts and intelligible meanings, is the principal object of the first volume—by far the better known—of the *Logical Investigations*. But, clearly, psychological acts and the contents they seek to grasp or to express could not be separated, like two worlds between which no communication could be established. It is in judgment, understood as psychological fact and subjective realization, that meaningful propositions are given to us. But, conversely, it is because it aims at an ideal signification that a psychological act is a judgment. Husserl has shown that one cannot elicit the logical from the psychological. He does not seek to derive from a world of pure logical essences the reality of experienced facts. One route alone remains possible: the one which, starting from logic and from psychology, will lead us to a basic discipline, differing at once from both, and in which they will have their common origin, their final justification, and the foundation of their reciprocal relations. The "neutral" [31] investi-

30. *Ibid.*, p. 111, § 32.
31. *Log. Unt.* (1st ed.), II, 4.

gations of this new domain will constitute the "phenomenology" to which the second volume of the *Logical Investigations* is principally consecrated. It bears the subtitle "Investigations of Phenomenology and the Theory of Knowledge." [32]

For Husserl it could not be a question of building immediately, and in some sense in the void, the theory of this original discipline. Nothing is more antipathetical to him than preconceived ideas or conceptual systems which do not directly translate a personal contact with concrete realities, with the "things themselves." Instead of defining phenomenology a priori with an illusory rigor, it is better to attack the problems in question, in this case, those problems posed in connection with the relation between facts and essences.

To begin with, it is thus necessary to study the multiple and complex relations that exist between a thought's *meaning* and its *expression,* the latter including the whole of the material signs that translate it, but also, on an intermediary level, the psychological events in which it is embodied.

It will also be necessary, as, for example, the Third and Fourth Investigations endeavor to do, to distinguish the autonomous contents of consciousness, which are sufficient unto themselves, from those which depend more or less closely on one another. How are these connections brought about, how are these implications drawn together, what sense is it proper to attribute to them? These are points one must have settled before approaching "the phenomenological explication of knowledge" [33] with which the entire Sixth Investigation is concerned.

If we seek to form an idea of phenomenology in its beginnings, after patient and minute preparatory work, it will appear to us as characterized first by a concern for pure description. It is this, in part, which compels Husserl to characterize his effort by use of the term "phenomenology," scarcely current in philosophical language. The "phenomenon" is not for him a more or less misleading appearance. Nor does it imply, as for Kant, the thought of a noumenon which would be its correlative; nor is it as yet the new, fully elucidated concept which the most recent

32. Halle a. d. Saale, 1901. In later editions the second volume was divided and published as two books.
33. *Log. Unt.* (1st ed.), II, 473 ff.

phenomenology will utilize, and which can be constituted only after the phenomenological reduction and that suspension of judgment which Husserl designates by the Greek noun epochē.[34] It is only what offers itself simply to the intellectual gaze, to pure observation. Phenomenology thus presents itself to us as a "purely descriptive [study] of the experiences of thought and of knowledge." [35]

But what is the nature of this observation without prejudice, of this direct intuition, for which the phenomenon is the sole matter to be studied? Its nature is to deal with meanings, to grasp the intelligible. It is not a matter of experiencing qualities, even less of grasping infra- or supra-intellectual realities,[36] but of understanding ideal relations. The point of view of *meaning*, which we will see Husserl constantly taking in the *Cartesian Meditations*, is already the one that prevails here. Certainly, Husserl preserves the rights and the place of sense experience, but his work as phenomenologist is to reflect on this knowledge, to understand its *sense* and to make explicit its essential conditions. When the phenomenologist studies the real data of consciousness in which judgments and logical reasonings appear, his aim is to obtain for us "the *comprehension* of these psychic experiences, to the extent to which it is necessary for us in order to give firm meanings to all the basic logical concepts." [37] Husserl's intuition is, then, undoubtedly not an intellectual intuition which would produce its own object but a grasp of the intelligible by the intelligence.

The second edition of the *Logical Investigations*, published in 1913, and so contemporary with *Ideen*, suppresses the term "descriptive" in the passage quoted at the top of this page. It would entail too great a risk of having phenomenology taken to be an

34. Edmund Husserl, "Krisis," p. 155; *Krisis*, p. 82; *Crisis*, p. 80.
35. *Log. Unt.* (1st ed.), II, 4.
36. Phenomenology is far removed from any mystical intuition. It wants to give to philosophy the nature of a rigorous science and therefore a science communicable with precision. "Profundity" (*Tiefsinn*) does not itself seem to be a philosophical quality, but "the sign of the chaos that true science must order into a cosmos . . . true science ignores all profundity . . . profundity is a matter of wisdom; clarity and conceptual distinction are the matter of rigorous theory" ("Philosophie als strenge Wissenschaft," *Logos*, I [1910], 339). (Hereafter cited as "'Phil. als str. Wiss.'")
37. *Log. Unt.* (1st ed.). II, 8. [Berger's italics.]

empirical study and thus confused with psychology. The new text specifies, on the contrary, that phenomenology studies the lived data of consciousness (*Erlebnisse*) "in their pure essential generality" [38] and not as data actually experienced, empirically grasped by conscious beings, within a nature.

Even in the first edition, and in spite of the imprecision unavoidable at the beginning of a new investigation, one does indeed see that phenomenology is something completely different from a particular form of psychology. If, to better understand it, one wants to compare it to a familiar branch of philosophy, it is with the theory of knowledge that analogies must be sought, but with a theory where any construction would be excluded. The expressions "theory of knowledge" and "phenomenology" are sometimes taken to be equivalent. Husserl speaks "of a foundation of pure logic from the point of view of the theory of knowledge, that is, of phenomenology." [39] "As is readily apparent, the concerns of phenomenological analysis," he writes again, "are not essentially different from those to which the fundamental questions of the theory of knowledge give rise." [40] The second edition slightly tones down the analogy, but without making it disappear, specifying that it is imposed only in the instance where the questions of the theory of knowledge are taken in their greatest generality. [41] This edition explains that it is a matter of "*understanding*" [42] how the "in-itself" of objectivity can come to a "representation" and, indeed, in knowledge, to "comprehension." [43] Husserl's most recent works, moreover, again take up this assimilation of phenomenology to the theory of knowledge, but they stress the particular sense which belongs to it as a result of its action on the transcendental level. [44]

The immediate intuition of intelligible realities, of essences— the *Wesensschau*—retained the attention of Husserl's first read-

38. *Log. Unt.* (2d ed.), I, 2.
39. *Log. Unt.* (1st ed.), II, 4.
40. *Ibid.*, p. 9.
41. *Log. Unt.* (2d ed.), II, Bk. 1, 8.
42. Italicized in the original.
43. *Log. Unt.* (2d ed.), II, Bk. 1, 8.
44. ". . . phenomenology seems to be rightly characterized also as *transcendental theory of knowledge*" (*CM*, p. 81).

ers, and for good reason. But if it led them to make a realist philosopher of Husserl, and if it still seems to many to be a mysterious operation, this is so precisely to the extent to which they all take a position of naïve dogmatism and ask themselves what kind of being is the being of essences, while phenomenology specifies that essences are nonreal and, overturning the traditional position, seeks the *sense* that must be given to being in general and to its different modalities.[45]

Habitual patterns of thought of Kantian origin are also quite troublesome when we try to place ourselves in the phenomenological perspective. We naturally identify passivity and sensibility and, on the other hand, assimilate comprehension to construction. With this starting point it is difficult for us to represent to ourselves an intuitive understanding without making it something analogous to sensibility. Yet intuition of essences, the *Wesensschau*, is not the apprehension of a thing or of an image, even of an original kind. It is purely in an analogous sense that we speak of vision here.[46] If we took the term literally, it would be as though, in reading Plato, we were to confuse the Idea of the Good with the sun.

Spontaneously dogmatic, we are also naturally empiricists. Intuition seems to us to be able to found only the contents that it actually offers us, like Condillac's sensation or Hume's idea. To see this watch, placed there on my table, is to be sunk in contemplation, perfect in itself: everything is there before me, given at once. My understanding will doubtless be able, subsequently, to construct problems with regard to the watch; for my eye there are no problems, only a presence. To be conscious of itself, it seems that the mind must either superimpose a new experience on sensible experience (and here arises the temptation to believe that by passing from external experience to internal experience we are dealing with metaphysics) or else feel its own action at the very moment it is performed. If idealism is identified beforehand with the activity of constructing, then intuition will seem to con-

45. Transcendental phenomenology will show that these meanings are constituted by transcendental subjectivity; it will pose for itself the problem of making this constitution explicit.

46. Eugen Fink, "Die phänom.," p. 329.

demn us definitively to realism. This alternative will vanish later on for phenomenology, when the new "dimension" of the transcendental is discovered. These oppositions will then be constituted inside the world, whose global sense is constituted by pure extraworldly subjectivity. But at the point where we now are, we can already escape the alternatives if we see in the *Wesensschau* the *comprehension* of a meaning.

And to comprehend, even in an intuitive manner, is not to vanish in the contemplation of an essence. It is to see, in the idea understood, all the other ideas it implies. Might it be said that this is contradictory, that it introduces discourse into intuition? This objection could only arise from the misunderstanding of the true relations among ideas and from the natural tendency of our mind to represent intellectual interiority to itself on the model of spatial exteriority. Moreover, as Levinas has well demonstrated,[47] Husserl does not seek above all to distinguish discourse from intuition as the simple from the complex. Intuition is not necessarily the grasp of a simple nature. It is what gives us a thing or an idea *primordially*, in itself.[48] It is first of all characterized by the *presence* of what we grasp. Intuition thus forms a genus of which sensible experience, on the one hand, or the vision of essences, on the other, will be the particular species.[49]

This is because, at every level, the life of the mind is characterized by its intentionality. First of all, consciousness could in no way be compared to a particular domain of being, which would have an inside and an outside. Its most profound nature is to be "intentional," that is, to be always directed toward a content which is heterogeneous to it. We will return at greater length to this notion in the next chapter, in connection with the interpretation of the *cogito*. We will then see how, after the phenomenological reduction, it permits an escape from the illusory alternatives of immanence and transcendence. Starting with Husserl's first works, the intentionality of consciousness invites us to abandon the conception of knowledge which identifies the subject and the

47. E. Levinas, *La Théorie de l'intuition dans la phénoménologie de Husserl* (Paris: Alcan, 1930), pp. 126–27.
48. Edmund Husserl, *Ideen*, p. 43.
49. *Ibid.*, pp. 37, 43.

object, an unjustified postulate in which Brunschvicg will rightly see "a superficial translation of the Cartesian *cogito*." [50]

But this "intention," this flight outside of self toward something else, is not of one kind only.[51] The way consciousness "sights" its object is not the same in judgment, in doubt, in desire, in fear, etc.[52] Moreover, each content of consciousness has horizons peculiar to itself; and in order that they may be understood, certain ideas call forth others toward which they tend by means of a particular "intention."

In order to better see in what these intentional implications consist, let us study an example.

In the third of his *Logical Investigations,* Husserl studies the example, borrowed from Stumpf, of the necessary connection between extension and the colored quality of a visual sensation. Stumpf notes that these two aspects of my perception are relatively independent. If the extended surface diminishes, it does not thereby become more or less red or more or less green. But let it decrease until it disappears, and the quality vanishes at the same time. So there is, he concludes, seconded by Husserl, a functional relation between quality and extension, which are thus found to be linked by nature.[53] As much could be said, Husserl continues, of the relation between the intensity and the quality of a sound: the intensity is something other than the tone, but they appear and disappear at the same time. What is important here is that it is not a matter of subjective connections.[54] By abstraction we can think of extension without considering color. But the idea of colored quality *implies* that of extended surface, and vice versa.

When I see a man's or a dog's head, I cannot perceive it without also seeing the background against which it stands out. But this impossibility is of an entirely different nature than that which forces us to posit the extension in positing the quality. What guides us here are the features belonging to the object of

50. L. Brunschvicg, *L'Idéalisme contemporain* (Paris: Alcan, 1921), p. 12.

51. *Log. Unt.* (1st ed.), II, 347–48.

52. Serrus has quite justly compared these distinctions with those made in Brunschvicg's study of the modality of judgment (*Etudes philosophiques,* II, No. 1 [May, 1928], pp. 10, 12).

53. *Log. Unt.* (1st ed.), II, 228 ff.

54. *Ibid.,* p. 235.

our thought itself: an extended surface without quality or, inversely, a color without extension would have *no* assignable *meaning* for us.

But these pure essences and these intentional implications, are they not, basically, of empirical origin? Are they not reducible to unconscious habits? This question challenges Husserl's entire philosophy. We can only indicate his answer. All of phenomenology will be its justification, that is, not only the published works, but especially the personal and prolonged effort by which the phenomenologist progressively tears himself away from the naturalist and empiricist prejudice, replaces dogmatic assertions with the progressive elucidation of meanings, and understands that all empirical sciences suppose essential cognitions and that, consequently, these could not come from experience by any process of induction whatever.

The essence of an object of thought, sensible or intellectual, its *eidos*,[55] is its particular way of being constituted, the whole of the essential predicates which constitute it and which "must belong to it so that other secondary and relative determinations can be attributed to it." [56] In order to extract these essences, which are at once *nonreal* and *concrete*, one does not depend on the constancy of observed relations in a multitude of different real cases; rather one must comprehend in an intuitive manner the necessary correlation of the elements. For this, it is doubtless necessary to make use of singular realities, but these enter only as examples. Thus, imaginary figures are just as suitable as real things to enable us to reach essences. We will arbitrarily modify—in our imagination—the form, the color, etc., of an object; we will vary the empirical elements of any cognition whatever, not to elaborate a general idea based on these individual givens but to directly see the universal in regard to sensible things. This methodical effort, which permits us to go beyond empirical generality to reach the essential necessity, glimpsed in its intelligibility, Husserl calls "eidetic reduction." [57]

55. *Ideen*, p. 6.
56. *Ibid.*, p. 9.
57. *Ideen*, p. 4. The *Ideas* do not give any concrete examples of eidetic reduction. Husserl had his students practice it as an exercise. He himself in his courses gave numerous examples of it. In the *Cartesian Meditations*

The analyses of the second volume of the *Logical Investigations* are to be understood as essential analyses, except where they deal with an expressly ontological theme (for example, in the Third and Fourth Investigations). They deal with neither psychological realities nor objective laws but with possibilities or pure necessities.[58]

But once one has "reduced" the facts in order to consider the essences, that is, when one has placed oneself on the level of comprehension, one realizes that there not only exist implications among essences, among particular meanings, but that *meaning* in general also implies, as "necessarily presupposed," [59] a pure subject to which it can offer itself.

The individual eidetic sciences, based on the intuition of essences, will determine the conditions which must be satisfied by a sound, a color, a memory, etc., in order to have the meaning peculiar to them. Husserl calls them "regional ontologies," [60] this term having with him no realist connotations. But it would be inexact to think that phenomenology exhausts itself in these "local" investigations. Husserl carries in himself the demand for absolute knowledge and for perfect rationality: philosophy must be a rigorous science, that is, a coherent system, built progressively on indubitable foundations [61] and capable of "forcing itself on every rational being." [62]

The regional eidetics bring to the fore little by little a completely original "region," that of consciousness.[63] On the other

---

(p. 70), he recalls, in connection with the phenomenological reduction, of which we will speak later, the features of the eidetic reduction which concerns us now. Husserl's first disciples, those who were his students at Göttingen, developed these eidetic investigations in particular; some will be found in the *Jahrbuch für Philosophie und phänomenologische Forschung*, which was published from 1913 to 1930. These early phenomenologists, however, mistook the means for the end, thinking that phenomenology resided entirely in the use of this method. As Fink justly notes, the simple description of regional essences could not be called a philosophy ("Was will . . . ," p. 28).

58. *Log. Unt.* (2d ed.), II, Bk. 2, 236.
59. *CM*, p. 26.
60. *Ideen*, p. 19.
61. "Phil. als str. Wiss.," p. 292.
62. *Ibid.*, p. 295.
63. *Ideen.*, pp. 87 ff.

hand, a true knowledge is not the juxtaposition of heterogeneous and irreducible givens. Essences grasped completely "separately," one from another, would be unintelligible. But, more profound than the conditions which make possible this group of objects or that series of qualities are the conditions which give a sense to the world, taken as a whole, with all the kinds of real beings or of ideal essences which are distinguished there. The first correlations to be discovered in the *Logical Investigations* are still "in the world," but they open the way to the discovery of the fundamental correlation which ties the entire world to the transcendental subject, the subject who bears the world within him "as an accepted sense." [64]

This idea of an ultimate relation to the subject was perhaps obscurely felt by Husserl when he called the investigations to which he wanted to dedicate himself "phenomenology." The "phenomenon" is neither the object of science nor the whole of nature. It is the world thought by a transcendental subject, what the *Cartesian Meditations* will later specify as *cogito qua cogitatum*.[65]

"The analysis of the value of logical principles leads to investigations centered on the subject," Husserl notes in 1929.[66] The *Logical Investigations* did in fact continually return to the central ideas of consciousness and subjectivity. Their transcendental origin remained to be discovered.

In his basic preoccupation with "sense," the theory of intentionality, and the procedure of "eidetic reduction," Husserl possessed the essential elements that permitted him to posit the "*cogito*" in the very way he posited it in his most recent works, that is, at the end of the original step that he calls "phenomenological reduction." [67] As Edith Stein quite justly notes, "Husserl

64. *CM*, p. 26.
65. *Ibid.*, p. 41.
66. *Logik*, p. 203.
67. "Reduction" is a general phenomenological process; it intervenes here in several different forms, of which the two principal forms are:
1. The eidetic reduction, which eliminates empirical elements and enables us to reach the *eidē*, the essences. It is of this one that we spoke on page 26.
2. The actual phenomenological reduction, which reduces—Husserl will even say "places in brackets"—the world and gives us the transcenden-

was able to arrive there without passing through Cartesian doubt." [68]

As a matter of fact, between the publication of the *Logical Investigations* in 1900–1901 and the appearance of the *Ideas* in 1913, Husserl's reflection was strongly influenced by Descartes's philosophy. The desire which animated his entire investigation, that of finding an absolute foundation for the sciences and for philosophy, his will to rid himself of all prejudices, his distance from philosophical disputes, and his avowed intention to neglect them in order to attack the problems directly, in themselves,[69] give him the attitude that was Descartes's. He will thus meditate a long time, not on the metaphysical propositions to which Descartes found himself led, but on the antecedents of the *cogito*, such as trey appear, for example, in the first two Meditations. Husserl will take up again, in his fashion, the universal doubt of the French philosopher; out of it he will pull the transcendental epochē and the phenomenological reduction.

tal ego. One could thus call it, in a more complete sense, transcendental phenomenological reduction. (See "Nachwort zu meinen *Ideen*," *Jahrbuch für Philosophie und phänomenologische Forschung*, XI [published separately in 1930], 544.) (Hereafter cited as " 'Nachwort.' ")

68. *La Phénoménologie* (report on the colloquium of September 12, 1932) (Juvisy, 1932), p. 46.

69. "Phil. als str. Wiss.," p. 340.

3 / The *Cogito* and the Phenomenological Reduction

DESCARTES, IN QUEST OF absolute knowledge, attempts to rid himself of the opinions he has received from his teachers or has found in books. He decides to submit all the cognitions which offer themselves to him, whether they come from his senses or from his understanding, to the test of a doubt which is as rigorous as possible. Rejecting as "absolutely false" anything in which he can "imagine the slightest doubt," [1] he intends to come to rest only upon a proposition that is impossible to doubt.

"I suppose, therefore," he writes, "that all the things I see are false; I persuade myself that nothing has ever existed of all that my lying memory presents to me; I feel I have no senses; I believe that body, shape, extension, motion and place are only fictions of my mind." [2]

Following Descartes, Husserl will surrender himself to methodical doubt. The Cartesian effort to establish a universal critique seems indispensable to him: such an examination is necessary at least "once in the life" of anyone for whom philosophy is something serious.[3]

Descartes wanted to exercise his doubt in an absolutely radical manner. Perhaps he did not realize his plan as completely as he hoped, but his intention is clear. Yet, carried along by his de-

1. *Discours de la Méthode*, part 4, ed. Adam and Tannery, VI, 31.
2. *Deuxième méditation*, Adam and Tannery, IX, 19.
3. Edmund Husserl, *CM*, p. 2. See also "Krisis," p. 151; *Krisis*, p. 77; *Crisis*, p. 76.

sire not to give way to prejudices and not to hold as true what is not certain, Descartes goes beyond this strict suspension of judgment, this epochē which is true doubt.[4] He overturns the theses he is considering, transforming their positing into their negation. The methods of reduction, with which the preparatory phenomenological investigations have familiarized us, will permit us to arrive at the result Descartes seeks, with greater certainty and without modifying in themselves, by completely suppressing their reality and their value, the propositions submitted to doubt. In eidetic reduction we do not suppress the existence of the object perceived any more than we held as illusory the psychological act by which we evoked an image or thought a category. But we *separated* the empirical intuition from the essential intuition. The former had been set aside, placed, so to speak, "in brackets," without being denied or destroyed. It remained there with the sense and the value that were its own. Would it not be possible to widen the area of application of this method and to make it coincide in this way with the universal doubt to which we want to surrender ourselves? This is what the phenomenological reduction proposes to do.[5]

In eidetic reduction we suspended the factual elements. It is now a matter of bracketing both the whole of facts and the whole of meanings (values, estimations, or essences), that is, this totality of which we are ourselves a part and which we call: the world. During this epochē, the world, placed in brackets, continues to offer itself to us as before;[6] its existence is not denied, and our previous cognitions are not assumed to be false. This

4. Edmund Husserl, *Ideen,* p. 54.
5. For transcendental phenomenology there are not two kinds of joint operations, one of which would be the epochē and the other the phenomenological reduction. These two terms signify the same spiritual movement; the accent is simply placed on different aspects, here on the character of irreducible residue which is that of the *cogito,* there on the attitude of suspension taken in respect to the entire world: "The fundamental phenomenological method of transcendental epochē, because it leads us back to this realm, is called transcendental-phenomenological reduction" (*CM,* p. 21).
6. "It goes on appearing, as it appeared before; the only difference is that I, as reflecting philosophically, no longer keep in effect (no longer accept) the natural believing in existence involved in experiencing the world—though that believing too is still there . . ." (*CM,* p. 20).

world is simply what appears to us and in connection with which we reserve our existential judgment: it is our *cogitatum.*[7]

What will we find after such a general reduction? Is our course even conceivable? When we move with all possible caution, taking care not to allow any element whatever of the world —fact or value—to emerge from the brackets, we see we are not left "confronting nothing."[8]

However, if we "reduce" everything that has a sense, will we not find, as residue, either the absurd or at least an insuperable mystery? This would be a defeat for Husserl, who intends to remain as far as possible from all mysticism and to deal with philosophy as a rigorous science.[9]

But meanings are not inert things which are self-sufficient and fully independent. Not only does each of them refer to a series of intentional complements which, in certain cases and, for example, in objects grasped in perception,[10] are developed indefinitely, but they all require a subject to whom they can offer themselves and in relation to whom they will be constituted as meanings. In other words, after having put aside everything that *has* a sense, we remain in the presence of that by which everything *receives* a sense: pure consciousness, the "I."

In this recognition of the thinking subject, we do not grasp a thought closed in on itself and constituting an original world over against the one we have reduced. What then becomes ours is "the universe of 'phenomena' in the (particular and also the wider) phenomenological sense,"[11] phenomenon meaning here the whole of the world thought by a subject insofar as this subject thinks it. The formula which will most precisely convey what phenomenological reduction yields will not be then the simple *cogito* in which the belief in the existence of spiritual substances, evident in Descartes, is revived.[12] Rather, it could be expressed as

7. The world, in the phenomenological attitude, is not an existence but a simple phenomenon (*CM*, p. 32).

8. *CM*, p. 20.

9. "The fundamental method of phenomenological philosophy is a strictly rational method" (Letter of Eugen Fink, May 11, 1936).

10. For the objects of external experience "no imaginable synthesis of this kind is completed as an adequate evidence" (*CM*, p. 62).

11. *CM*, pp. 20–21.

12. "The subjects of all acts are indeed truly understood as being sub-

follows: *"ego—cogito—cogitata qua cogitata."* [13]

What intervenes here to separate Husserl's position from that of Descartes is the fundamental notion of the intentionality of consciousness. The "I" who remains after the phenomenological reduction is not a separate reality that, in a mysterious and somewhat accidental manner, would have to come into contact with an "external world." Psychology and metaphysics are burdened by all the pseudo-problems that have arisen from this naïve conception. Now on the one hand this notion rests on the constant confusion which Descartes was unable to overcome between the transcendental subject and the soul; and, on the other hand, it rests on the idea of a substantial soul [14] whose thoughts would be its modifications.

Let us recall that for Husserl, on the contrary, the very essence of consciousness is to be directed toward something other than itself: that is the life proper to it. To say simply "I think" has thus no meaning.[15] Placed in brackets, the world must remain there, as phenomenon, in order for the *cogito* to have meaning: "the transcendental ego is what it is solely in relation to intentional objects." [16] In addition to purely psychological intentionality, which causes a thinking being to seek objects outside himself, there will be superimposed transcendental intentionality, in which the "I" thinks the "World." The latter will, in turn, be extended to a third form, constitutive intentionality, which we will mention later in sketching the plan of the tasks imposed upon

stances . . . but not therefore as bodies" (Descartes, *Réponse aux troisièmes objections*, Adam and Tannery, IX, 136). And he continues: "All logicians, and almost everyone with them, usually say that among substances some are spiritual and others corporeal." And again: "It is certain that thought cannot exist apart from a thinking being, nor in general can any accident or act exist apart from a substance of which it be the act" (*ibid.*).

13. "Krisis," p. 152; *Krisis*, p. 79; *Crisis*, p. 77.

14. "Sum igitur praecise tantum res cogitans, id est mens, sive animus, sive intellectus, sive ratio . . ." (*Deuxième méditation*, ed. Adam and Tannery, X, 27).

15. "The word intentionality signifies nothing else than this universal fundamental property of consciousness: to be consciousness *of* something; as a *cogito*, to bear within itself its *cogitatum*" (*CM*, p. 33).

16. *CM*, p. 65 (modified); cf. *Méditations cartésiennes*, translated from the German by Gabrielle Peiffer and Emmanuel Levinas (Paris, 1931; 2d ed., 1947), p. 55. (Hereafter cited as *"Méd. cart."*)

the phenomenologist after the phenomenological reduction. Unpublished manuscripts show that Husserl carried the constitutive interpretation of the world quite far; but the texts accessible to the public still give us very little.

Psychological intentionality describes a human knowledge that is purely receptive. *Transcendental intentionality* is somewhat neutral. *Constitutive intentionality* accounts for the origin of the world; it is creative, if we consider the word "creative" in an analogous sense without making it correspond to the idea of production comparable to that effected in nature. However, these three concepts do not designate three types of truly separate acts but only three degrees of the *same* intentional life, as it is more or less profoundly understood.[17]

In the same way, beneath the psychological "I," engaged in the world and not yet torn away from the natural attitude, phenomenological reduction sights the transcendental "I." But it is itself the act of a deeper "I," of a spectator who watches, without participating in the cognition of the world, how the latter offers itself to the transcendental subject.[18] Yet, these three "I's" are no more separate from one another than are the three degrees of intentionality we have enumerated. When man is still immersed in his primitive naïveté, he is *already* a transcendental "I," but he is not yet aware of it.[19]

We must make several further clarifications concerning the notion of intentionality and the meaning of philosophical terms that apply to it and that have a special sense in phenomenology.

For the phenomenologist, psychological consciousness, man's soul, is in the "world." Psychology, which takes this consciousness as its special object, unfolds inside the natural attitude, when it proceeds a priori as well as when it employs inductive methods. To use Husserl's terminology, we will say that the object of psychology is *regional*.[20] The modifications of this psychological consciousness are its *immanent* contents. But in these immanent

17. E. Fink, "Die phänom.," p. 373.
18. *Ibid.*, p. 355.
19. One cannot help thinking here of the philosophy of the Upanishads. Atman is Brahman for the mad man and for the wise man, but the wise man alone has understood this supreme truth.
20. E. Fink, "Die phänom.," p. 358.

states consciousness grasps *transcendent* objects which constitute their meaning, or toward which its intention is directed according to its variable modes (cognition, evaluation, belief, etc.). It is in this sense that the *Ideas* speak of a correlation between the immanent and the transcendent.[21] A few pages earlier,[22] Husserl had specified that he was going to develop a series of considerations in which he would place himself *prior* to the phenomenological reduction, that is, he would again take the natural attitude. He specifies later that actually he has not abandoned this attitude.[23] These terms are understood, then, solely in relation to psychological consciousness: the transcendent, which is opposed to human consciousness as being by essence nonpsychic, remains, however, *in the world* [24] and receives its meaning only in relation to transcendental subjectivity.[25] To borrow an expression from René Le Senne which seems particularly apt,[26] we will say that, for Husserl, the thing in itself is nothing other than the thing-in-itself-as-thought (thought, of course, by the transcendental subject).

Realism is thus correct in affirming the transcendence of real things in relation to consciousness, since it also places itself in the natural attitude, which opposes the soul to its body and to bodies. In the vast cosmos man is only a miserably limited being,[27] and one must agree that it is laughable to reduce the being of the entire world to nothing but a human dream—as subjective idealism would attempt to do—since man in turn is only a fragment of the world. The philosopher finds himself caught in a vicious circle if he does not raise himself to the level of transcendental subjectivity.

The first form of intentionality consists, then, in the fact that, *in the world,* man, through his lived psychological states (*Erleb-*

21. *Ideen,* pp. 67 and 68.
22. *Ibid.,* p. 60.
23. *Ibid.,* p. 69.
24. E. Fink, "Die phänom.," p. 361.
25. "Every imaginable sense, every imaginable being, whether the latter is called immanent or transcendent, falls within the domain of transcendental subjectivity, as the subjectivity that constitutes sense and being" (*CM,* p. 84).
26. René Le Senne, *Obstacle et valeur* (Paris: Aubier, 1934), pp. 19 ff.
27. E. Fink, "Die phänom.," p. 377.

nisse), seeks objects whose entire meaning implies that they are transcendent in relation to him. Reflecting upon this problem teaches us that traditional psychology, falsified by metaphysical notions of substance and accident, should properly be replaced by an *intentional psychology*. The latter will remain, however, entirely distinct from phenomenology. Both, certainly, will be developed in a parallel manner, beginning necessarily with the *ego cogito;* [28] but intentional psychology remains in the world, where it must distinguish the subjective from the objective, being-for-us from being-in-itself, or, in other words, the representation of the world from the real world (without its being a question, however, of things in themselves, which would be imitated by subjective images); phenomenology, on the contrary, develops its analyses starting from a transcendental *cogito,* which it must first elicit and in which an "extraworldly" subject turns itself toward the whole of the world and there finds its soul with its flow of consciousness as well as its transcendent objects.

Can the phenomenological reduction, which gives us access to the entire domain proper to phenomenology [29] by leading us to the *cogito,* be considered a logical process? Is it a kind of reasoning? Yes and no. Phenomenology is indeed a method, and one that wants to be strictly rational; but in no instance does it create its object. It does not construct the consequence with the premises, as does deduction. It does not limit itself, like the analytical method, to separating previously existing elements. It attempts to carry us from the given to what it implies and to that by which it will itself be explained. But it is never other than a matter of "affirming" insufficiencies or justifications. The methodical precautions and the expositional procedures serve only to "turn the eye of the soul" toward the correct direction, as Socrates tells us in the *Republic.* It is after the manner of Plato that Husserl seeks to show us how we must lay hold of ourselves in order to elicit a knowledge that we already possess virtually but which is obscured

---

28. *CM,* p. 38.

29. *Ideen,* p. 59. Answering for Husserl to recent criticisms, Fink specifies that "the fundamental method of the phenomenological philosophy of Edmund Husserl is uniquely and exclusively phenomenological reduction" ("Die phänom.," p. 322).

by our interest in sensible things. In connection with sensations that awaken its perplexity,[30] the soul is invited to recognize the original nature of ideas. Without condemning the practical applications of the sciences, the philosopher studies them only as a preparation for the dialectic. We can say, in an analogous fashion, that the interest of *eidetic reductions* does not reside in the progress they can allow, if we apply them to this or that investigation in particular, but in the practice they give us in detaching ourselves from spatiotemporal experience and in the exercise of a dawning spiritual freedom.

But, if the sciences prepare the way for the dialectic, they still essentially differ from it. And so, too, eidetic reductions in relation to the phenomenological reduction. Already, in connection with the former, it would be imprecise to confuse the general process of reduction with a psychological act of abstraction: what we intuitively grasp after an eidetic reduction is something *concrete*, that is, in the sense that Husserl understands it, an essence which possesses its own sufficiency.[31] We must always understand that we are speaking in terms of the phenomenologist. An *abstraction*, on the contrary, is only an essence void of autonomy (*ibid.*).

It would be even more imprecise to think of abstraction in connection with phenomenological reduction: the latter raises itself from nature to the subject who thinks it and, in the final analysis, founds it, constitutes it. Now, by abstraction, one can never draw from nature anything but the natural.[32] The expressions used in the *Ideas* can contribute to erroneous impressions on this point: the *cogito* is presented there as a phenomenological "residue"; it constitutes a special ontological "region." [33]

These terms would be inadequate if taken literally. It is only because it is a question of preliminary considerations [34] that Husserl uses them and because it is first a matter of suggesting to his readers, who have no notion of it, the character of an original step that no description can rigorously convey. Hence, one must

30. Plato, *The Republic*, Book VII, 523c–524d.
31. *Ideen*, p. 29.
32. *Ibid.*, p. 95.
33. *Ibid.*, p. 59.
34. *Ibid.*, p. 95.

use the simplest concepts, those with which the reader would be most likely to be familiar. It is only later, when the concrete and personal effort required by the phenomenological reduction will have been initiated, that one's first impressions will be able to be rectified. It will then be seen that the phenomenological reduction has properly no regional character and that it would have to be said to "return" to the subject; thus one cannot use terms, like *Ausschaltung,* which make one think of elements set aside in order to find what, like a residue, had been mixed in them.[35]

These remarks on vocabulary could be pursued indefinitely. They express a difficulty inherent in phenomenology, one which arises from having to reveal with words "which are of the world" the intentional existence of a transcendental subject, located outside the world, although related to it.[36] All the concepts we can employ take their immediate sense from nature. They are loaded with spontaneous associations, all of which evoke things in the world or natural acts. Any expression is hence necessarily inadequate. It will have only the value of an analogous indication, useful only for those who have themselves undergone transcendental experiences.

It is not just the difficulty of finding perfectly exact terms which renders insufficient the exposition we have given of the phenomenological reduction: it is in particular its concrete and personal character. Since it is an original spiritual process that one must accomplish oneself, what can best be done to facilitate its realization is to suppress, or at the very least to indicate, the obstacles which might hinder the conversion it requires. We can do this, in particular, by saying *what* the phenomenological reduction *is not,* which will prevent our getting lost along the way or believing the goal is reached when the essential has not been accomplished.

It must be recognized that Husserl himself does not offer easy access to transcendental phenomenology to those who do not spontaneously feel inclined to assume the attitudes it proposes to us. Husserl works more than he explains. Moreover, he writes

35. E. Fink, "Die phänom.," p. 366.
36. On a lower level, the *Logical Investigations* already indicate how difficult it was to express "acts" by words habitually used to signify "things" (*Log. Unt.,* Part II, Introduction [1st ed.], II, 11).

solely to say what he sees. Then it is up to each of us to see for himself: if we do not see "ideas," for example, it is because we are affected "with a kind of spiritual blindness" [37] due to our prejudices.

Husserl did not publish the important manuscripts in which his concrete approach to the *cogito* is expounded. Transcendental phenomenology is set forth in the *Ideas;* but only the first volume has appeared,[38] and we have emphasized its in many respects preliminary character. Transcendental phenomenology is presented in a more complete fashion in the *Cartesian Meditations,* but in an extremely condensed form, since in 140 pages Husserl deals not only with the access to the transcendental but also with the problems of the phenomenological philosophy [39] which arise after the phenomenological reduction. The author's attempt to thus condense—and to explain in four lectures [40]—the essential aspects of his doctrine leads to a valuable overview, but one which gives us only a general and necessarily abstract outline.

Hence we will try to interpret the *Ideas* and the *Cartesian Meditations* by referring their precise texts to the intellectual movement they attempt to convey. We will be aided by short writings in which Husserl himself comments on his doctrine,[41] as well as by those of Eugen Fink, particularly the long article which appeared under his signature in *Kantstudien* [42] in answer

37. *Ideen,* p. 41.
38. [The second part of the *Ideen—Phänomenologische Untersuchungen zur Konstitution—*was published in 1952 (twelve years after Berger's *Cogito*) by Martinus Nijhoff, The Hague, as the fourth volume of *Edmund Husserl: Gesammelte Werke* in the *Husserliana* collection; and the third part, *Die Phänomenologie und die Fundamente der Wissenschaften,* appeared in 1952 as the fifth volume.—Translator.]
39. E. Fink, who seeks to unify the phenomenological vocabulary, reserves the title of phenomenology to the transcendental reflections which elicit the *cogito* (principally, those we are studying here). He calls "phenomenological philosophy" the study of traditional problems, taken up again after reduction, on new foundations.
40. Husserl delivered at the Sorbonne, on February 23 and 25, 1929, four lectures in German on the "Introduction to Transcendental Phenomenology." Their text, developed and quite extensively revised by the author, was translated into French by Peiffer and Levinas, and forms the *Méditations cartésiennes.*
41. Notably in "Nachwort zu meinen *Ideen*" and in *Die Krisis der europäischen Wissenschaften und die transzendentale Phänomenologie.*
42. E. Fink, "Die phänom."

to the criticisms addressed to phenomenology by Zocher and Kreis. In a preface written for this study, Husserl states that he finds his thought very precisely expressed here and that he could acknowledge as his own all its assertions.[43] Thus we can rely in all confidence upon the important analyses that Fink performs here.

It is inevitable that the same doctrine should change its apparent character slightly when presented by two different philosophers, even if they be master and disciple. Husserl speaks more as a logician. Technical and difficult, his style is willfully sparse. A younger man, Fink conveys to us in a much more impassioned manner and with more emotion the intellectual movement that constitutes phenomenology. Even the difference in their manner of rendering an identical topic will help us understand its meaning better.

Before using this double instruction to help us understand the phenomenological reduction clearly, we must warn against an initial mistake: one which would have the reduction discarded as a simple verbal construction, unconsciously employing mere habits of speech. The *cogitatum* refers to the *cogito*, the object to the subject, the world thought to the "I" who thinks it: here, there would be only word play or at least banalities. Everything is given beforehand, by the very way in which the first of the two referential notions is conceived.

We acknowledge that there is an immediate and evident inference from the world to the subject. But this does not connect two abstract terms, two notions: it is still in the world that rhetoric develops. What is effected in phenomenological reduction is less the passage from the object to the subject than the realization of the world as object, as phenomenon—*qua cogitatum*.[44] It is, if one likes, an analysis: there is a more profound category than that of being and nonbeing, that of the object as thought. But, in connection with all the particular problems upon which one can reflect, it is an indefinitely repeated analysis. It is also something entirely other than the assertion, introduced by considerations of pure form, since become deplorably banal, that

43. *Ibid.*, p. 320.
44. *CM*, pp. 31, 32, 33.

it is "impossible to objectify the subject without contradiction." [45] It is understandable that realist philosophers or positivists with a scientific background have somewhat disdainfully remained aloof from these verbal artifices.

To think the world as a phenomenon, to elicit the subject from the world as phenomenology intends to do, is far from an easy thing. Not only are our intellectual practices opposed to it, but our sensible attachments as well: the phenomenological reduction has moral conditions.[46] It implies an uncommon detachment. Not that the phenomenologist is uninterested in human problems. Quite the contrary. But he considers that they can be undertaken in what is at once a fruitful and a salutary manner only if we do not renounce the legitimate ambitions of reason, if we do not abandon the pursuit of solidly founded truth. Now, this can be established only if we perform transcendental reflection and if we distinguish in itself the absolute "I," not only from the body in terms of which its sensations are organized, but also from the soul in which it expresses itself and from its flow of consciousness.

After eidetic reduction, which separates the region of essences from that of facts, after philosophical reduction,[47] which extends the epochē to theories and to systems,[48] the phenomenological reduction, which sets aside both facts and essences, places the entire world in brackets and uncovers the necessary character of the subject. In so doing, it makes us understand the unity of the world [49] but makes us see, too, that "the whole world and all that exists generally is for me only what 'holds' for me, that is, it exists for me only as *cogitatum* of my changing and, while changing, interconnected *cogitationes*." [50] Hence, what is im-

45. E. Fink, "Was will . . . ," p. 26.
46. Phenomenological reduction "is nothing like an intellectual action, 'purely' theoretical and which would bind to nothing. It is a spontaneous spiritual step *which grasps man in his entirety*" (E. Fink, "Was will . . . ," p. 18).
47. *Ideen*, p. 33.
48. Husserl does not pretend to be ignorant of earlier philosophies. He situates himself in respect to them and recognizes what he owes to his predecessors. But, in his personal meditation, he "suspends" theories in order to turn himself toward the things themselves. Cf. *Ideen*, p. 35.
49. *CM*, p. 140.
50. *Méd. cart.*, pp. 31–32. Cf. *CM* (Cairns), p. 140.

portant here is not a kind of abstract crossing from the object to the subject but the concrete, lived realization that the entire sense of the world is to be the *cogitatum* of a subject which transcends it.

This recognition, which must be prepared by reflection pursued over a long period of time and by sincere doubt, appears, however, in itself as a new element, a gratuitous event. Actually, it is indeed in a rather sudden manner that, in 1905, the idea of the phenomenological reduction presented itself to Husserl's mind.[51] After the publication of the Logical Investigations, he was concerned with understanding the final nature of the existing relations "between the unity of the object and a subjective system of intentional multiplicities."[52] By the phenomenological reduction and through the solution of difficulties raised by the apparent paradoxes of the transcendental, intentionality revealed its character to the very depths of pure subjectivity, by which every justification is effected.

As men, we are in the world. Moreover, even as subjects and before transcendental reflection reveals us to ourselves, we are turned toward the world. It alone do we know[53]—its things, its facts, its values, its multiple meanings. To grasp the self and "my life"[54] requires that we move out of this natural attitude, which is not false but simply naïve.

Here a difficulty arises: naïveté is evident only to one who has freed himself from it. It is only when the phenomenological reduction has elicited the pure "I" that we see the natural illusion to which we had formerly submitted. Before the reduction we do not have the impression of being enclosed inside a limited area, deprived of any real consistency. We are in the cave without knowing it—"befangen und nicht gefangen."[55] Knowing that we have nothing before us but shadows presupposes a knowledge of real objects.[56] A slave must have some idea of freedom to understand the constraint imposed by his chains.

51. E. Fink, "Die phänom.," p. 321.
52. E. Fink, letter of April 18, 1937.
53. *Ideen*, p. 7.
54. *CM*, p. 25.
55. Remark of Edmund Husserl.
56. E. Fink, "Was will . . . ," p. 17.

So, for those who are in the natural attitude, there is, strictly speaking, no reason to go beyond the world, to conceive an "extra-worldly" term. Even the inferences found in meanings could not suffice here: they are limited to referring us indefinitely from term to term and from idea to idea, just as genetic research is destined to go back endlessly from cause to cause. For the phenomenologist, there will be an essential problem after the reduction: that of the origin of the world.[57] Before the reduction, there were only problems of origin *in* the world. The term "origin" has, moreover, entirely different meanings in the two cases. If we seek the "motives" that move men to effect the phenomenological reduction, that is, to bracket the whole world, with its real events and its ideal values, it will be impossible to uncover any: the phenomenological reduction is "unmotivated." [58]

It is not without reason that Plato explained the knowledge of Ideas by recollection; they could not be derived from images, which are less worthy; one can only remember them when they happen to present themselves. In an analogous fashion, Husserl thinks that we have in principle, or if one prefers, potentially, an awareness of our transcendental subjectivity but that we do not always manage to make it explicit. The determinative reason for the reduction is not below it, in the world. It is above it, in what constitutes its end: pure subjectivity. When we practice the epochē, it is not to resolve a problem in the world, which would be given to us in advance,[59] since it is precisely a matter of leaving aside, of placing in brackets, everything that is part of the world, including our philosophical preoccupations. Questioning the phenomenologist about the motives we may have, in following him, to make the reduction closely resembles the questions put to the sage by those who ask what interest one finds in being disinterested.

In other words, we could say that the phenomenological reduction "presupposes itself." [60] This is basically the scandal of every conversion: it seems necessary, afterwards, to those who have been converted, but it seems paradoxical to those who have

57. E. Fink, "Die phänom.," p. 344.
58. Ibid., pp. 344, 346, 382.
59. Ibid., p. 344.
60. Ibid., p. 346.

not yet surrendered themselves. This is because the phenomeno-logical reduction is not a possibility of man; it is a possibility of the transcendental ego we truly are without knowing it. It is im-possible for the man we believe ourselves to be, but it constitutes the elementary act of our most intimate personality.[61] Its true motives lie in the depths of transcendental subjectivity.[62]

This permits us to understand two difficulties that stop us at the entrance to phenomenology—or, more precisely, the double aspect assumed by a single difficulty.

Phenomenology is an explication by finality in the strongest sense of the term. Its distance from all that is mere "construc-tion" expresses succinctly its aversion to explaining the superior by the inferior. Little by little, superior levels are discovered; they are not "manufactured," and an act is elucidated more by the in-tention that animates it than by the elements it employs. When Husserl seeks to elicit the essential idea of logic,[63] for example, he will not do it by grouping in one class the common features of the works produced by logicians, but by investigating their com-mon and living intention, the goal toward which they strive—a goal which none of them has yet managed to reach but which still gives a sense and a value to their attempts. Husserl will take the same attitude in regard to his own works: far from explaining the phenomenological reduction by eidetic reduction, which precedes it, one must do the opposite. This is why the phenome-nological reduction is not a reasoning, that is, a procedure of the mind which, starting from certain givens, asserts a conclusion that follows, whether it is seen in the premises by analysis or con-structed by means of previously known truths. It is not an inven-tion but a discovery.

This is nevertheless rather puzzling. To acknowledge that what we are concerned with at a particular point of the investiga-tion is explained, not by what precedes, which we could freely make use of, but by what follows, which we do not yet possess, means prohibiting any definitive explanation: phenomenology will be able to clearly state what it is only at the very end of its advances. Husserl does not seek to hide the constantly provi-

61. E. Fink, letter of May 11, 1936.
62. *Ibid.*
63. Edmund Husserl, *Logik,* p. 9.

sional character of what he offers us. He even sees this as the dignity and solidity of his philosophy. But if he thus surrenders all claims to providing us with separate results, valid once and for all, he does invite us to follow him in making the necessary effort to raise ourselves to a superior level: this doctrine of intentionality expands into an intellectual dynamic.

Perhaps this will help us understand why Husserl was in so little hurry to publish his manuscripts and so easily tolerated it that those whose publication he had begun remained uncompleted: it is because clarification is found in the changing perspective which follows the deepening of the investigation; and, as the mind is always in advance of its works, at every instant it grasps the insufficiencies of the preceding attempts at explication; it sees their origin in the naïveté of which it is now free, and it feels little desire to resume reflections it knows can lead nowhere.

Phenomenology is thus presented as a series of successive stages of knowledge.[64] Each moment of reflection enlightens the preceding moments; but one could not exactly say that it requires further stages. These will always conserve an air of gratuitousness in connection with the present reflection. The feeling of insufficiency that overwhelms us with its uneasiness on the lower levels of knowledge comes less from the internal inconsistency essential to them, but which we are unable to unmask, than from the nostalgic anticipation of the clarity yet to be acquired.

Eidetic reduction raised us one degree. The phenomenological reduction made us cross to a second stage. But the realization of the *cogito,* to which it leads, will not at once bring us the solution to all our problems. The "I" itself has not yet been truly elucidated. It is constitutive phenomenology that will give us the sense of both the transcendental subject and the world with all its facts and values. Have we arrived here at the end? We could not determine this a priori. Let us patiently surrender ourselves to the subtle and difficult constitutive analyses which we will try to outline in the next chapter.

If the phenomenologist cannot imagine beforehand the evidence his later meditations will offer to him, it is just as difficult

64. E. Fink, "Die phänom.," p. 371.

for him to communicate to others the cognitions he may already have acquired. In the field of his own experience, the evidence is certainly not lacking. But how can it be revealed to those who are not yet sensitive to it? To limit ourselves to the problem which is the object of our study—the transcendental *cogito*—transcendental phenomenology must in some sense go back into the world if it is to be able to reach those who believe themselves still imprisoned there.[65] By reduction, the phenomenologist has broken the natural tie that allowed him to enter into relation with his fellows. To restore that tie, he must allow the purity of his regard to be contaminated. He must again take up points of contact with the man still in his natural naïveté—that is, with the dogmatist. He will not, however, himself fall back into dogmatism, for at the moment when he reassumes the natural attitude, he understands its transcendental meaning.

But it is precisely this meaning that escapes the dogmatist. It is impossible, consequently, to tell him, as in a precise message, what it is that one knows and he does not know. One can only make preliminary recommendations, furnish provisional indications.[66]

This is a new reason to recognize that it is impossible to provide a rigorous and complete account of phenomenological reduction.

65. *Ibid.*, p. 381.
66. *Ibid.*, p. 382.

4 / Transcendental Evidence

OUR PRECEDING CHAPTER ended with a negative conclusion: the pure subject, the transcendental ego, proposed by
phenomenology as the final point of our effort, is incompatible
with the precise descriptions we would like to give it at the start.
All the attributes we could apply to it would be inadequate because they would have been borrowed from the "world," whereas
the ego is "extraworldly." Moreover, the very step by which we
must manage to grasp this ultimate reality in its purity is in
some sense ineffable.[1] What is said to us concerning it remains
analogical and has only the value of an entirely external invitation, an exhortation to make for ourselves a journey in advance
of which nothing really precise can be said to those who have
not yet made it. To further deepen the feeling of mystery and
uneasiness that we cannot help experiencing, we are not prom-
ised at the end a marvelous and immediate revelation, a definitive illumination: phenomenological reduction does not guide us
toward a being whose general structure, at least formally, is
known in advance.[2] It ends "in the obscurity" (*ibid.*) of something completely unknown to us. It opens a new world for us,
one yet to be explored. Far from giving us a complete explana-

1. In the sense "that it cannot be presented by means of simple sentences of the natural attitude. It can be spoken of only by transforming
the natural function of language" (E. Fink, letter of May 11, 1936).
2. E. Fink, "Die phänom.," p. 367.

tion, it makes us see a complex of new problems, unknown to us initially.

In the pages already devoted to phenomenological reduction, we have attempted to show that it could not be viewed as a dialectical construction, which would be effected openly, yet abstractly and conceptually. Now we must reject the opposing interpretation, which, in order to free phenomenology from verbal trickery, would make it a kind of mystical activity or esoteric discipline.

Indeed, in coming to this conclusion, we would have lost sight of Husserl's profound intention. He proposes neither to agitate nor to edify; according to him, philosophy realizes its true mission only if it has the quality of a "rigorous science." [3] When we said that the phenomenological reduction was a step each of us must in fact accomplish for himself in order to understand its nature and its range, that in no way affected either the intelligible character of phenomenological teaching or its universality. Although in an entirely different realm, it is a precaution analogous to that we give to students in telling them that geometry consists in redoing, each for himself, certain conceptual constructions and certain "logical verifications" [4] and not in looking at figures or in memorizing theorems. The fact that mathematical reasonings are incorporated into the psychological life of particular individuals does not change the ideal, atemporal, and perfect nature of the demonstrations. The earliest phenomenological studies have indeed taught us to make this distinction.

As it is necessary to reduce facts by a personal act in order to see essences, it is also necessary to reduce the world by a different but equally personal act in order to discover our ego. The sense of the *eidē* is indifferent to our behavior as an individual; so, too, with the truth of the *cogito* and the reality of the constitutions which are effected in pure consciousness. It is the "point-of-view philosophy," the philosophy that unfolds through grandiose intuitions of the universe, "which teaches as does wisdom: person to person." [5] Besides how could we think, without contradiction, that the phenomenological reduction is a procedure which the

3. Edmund Husserl, "Philosophie als str. Wiss.," *passim*.
4. E. Goblot, *Traité de logique* (Paris: Colin, 1918), p. 165, § 102.
5. "Phil. als str. Wiss.," p. 338.

master, by his personal influence, could enable the disciple to effect, since it consists in holding the entire world in suspension, with all those found there, including my master and myself!

Nor is the phenomenological reduction a series of intellectual acts which would create their object. Husserl, who always remained, as he was at the beginning, the adversary of subjective idealism, is at no less a distance from the magical idealism of the romantics. He is attempting a purely rational undertaking where persons have no right to intervene. Philosophy wants to be a true science, and "science is impersonal." [6]

The difficulties we may find here come largely from habits of thought whose origin must be sought principally in Kant's philosophy—habits which cause us great difficulty in recognizing the intuitive nature of the understanding, as Husserl asks us to do.

Phenomenological intuition is the immediate grasp of a reality which offers itself to us "in person." [7] This reality, which is directly apprehended, can no more be constructed than a simple quality like blue can be defined. All that is possible is to indicate the conditions to be fulfilled for the intuition to become possible. Maintaining that the phenomenological reduction is a personal step amounts, then, to saying that we lack the intuition of the *cogito* if we are not effectively doing what is necessary to make it accessible.

All the commentaries, so penetrating and so useful, that Fink gives us in his article in *Kantstudien* neither simply repeat Husserl's works nor do they disturb the balance of the doctrine: it remains strictly rational. Yet, while Husserl shows in what way the "I" presents itself in evident intuition as constituting the world, Fink dispels the misunderstandings which prevent our obtaining the corresponding intuitions. Husserl speaks to those who can follow him. Fink, precisely because he is answering critics, turns toward those who have not followed. The former describes what he sees. The latter reminds us that before judging whether phenomenological descriptions are exact, we must each perform the proper conversion.

6. *Ibid.*, p. 339.
7. Edmund Husserl, *Ideen*, pp. 7–36; E. Fink, "Die phänom.," p. 366.

In order to follow Husserl and to discover a positive meaning for phenomenology, we must have effected the phenomenological reduction. Suppose that we have succeeded in this. We have neither destroyed nor denied this physical and psychophysical world in which we live but have put it in brackets. At the same time we have enclosed in this reserved area all the ideal individualities constituted by our value judgments: sciences, techniques, arts, religions, morals, social forms, codes of law, etc.—in a word, all the manifestations of culture.[8] We have also set aside eidetic sciences—the formal ones like logic and the material ones like geometry and pure physics.[9] We have held in suspension our existential assertions, not only when they involve worldly givens, not only when they concern divine transcendence,[10] but even when they apply to the purely immanent content of our flow of consciousness: we have ourselves been "reduced," insofar as we are men participating in the world. What remains before our regard? The transcendental ego and the life proper to it. A new field of investigation is opened to us: the "field of transcendental experience."[11]

The term "experience" employed here by Husserl, and used by him on numerous occasions, merits attention. The entire initial effort of phenomenology was directed against empiricism, and now, after having suspended at once the results of all sciences based on facts and all sciences based on essences, we fall back on experience. Is this not returning to positions we previously demonstrated to be untenable? By making everything rest on the unshakable certainty that the "experience" of the self brings us, do we not end in psychologism?

In fact Husserl's use of the term "experience" is by no means casual: "[The] phenomenological epochē lays open to me, the meditating philosopher," he writes in the *Cartesian Meditations*, "*an infinite realm of being of a new kind,* as the sphere of a new kind of experience: transcendental experience."[12] And, in the *Logic:* "It is this (experience) that tells me then: I experience

8. *Ideen*, p. 108.
9. *Ibid.*, pp. 111–15.
10. *Ibid.*, p. 110.
11. Edmund Husserl, *CM*, p. 27.
12. *Ibid.*

myself in a primary originality." [13] The *Appendix to the Ideas,*
dating from 1930, specifies that the author wanted to present
there the fundamental principles "of a science that corresponds
to a new *field of experience,* which belongs to it in particular,
that of transcendental subjectivity." [14] Many similar quotations
could be found. The transcendental experience at issue here can
even serve as the basis for an eidetic science that will study the
structure of its region, just as the experiences presented to us in
the world can do. In the same way as the spatial structure of
physical objects provides the means for geometry as an eidetic
discipline, we will be able to discover "a *universal apodictically
experienceable structure* of the Ego [*Ich*]" [15] which will be the
object of a transcendental eidetics.

Is the *cogito* then a fact [16] which would possess only the
property of being irreducible and which would thus merit a
special place in our experience? We would then simply be re-
minded of its originary power by reserving for it the epithet
"transcendental" to distinguish it from the facts of sensible experience. [17] The comparison between these two types of fact is
further intensified when Husserl tells us that the *cogito* is given
to us in a perception. [18]

The terms used should not mislead us. The mobility of vocabulary is not the least of the problems that must be overcome in
order to understand phenomenology. We would run into numerous contradictions if we were to apply Husserlian expressions
strictly. Contrary to general opinion, nothing less resembles a
scholasticism in which each term would have, once and for all,
a perfectly determined meaning than does phenomenology. It is
dogmatism that appears so sure of the future and does not
hesitate to bind it with irrevocable definitions. Husserl wants to

13. Edmund Husserl, *Logik,* p. 206.
14. Edmund Husserl, "Nachwort," p. 552.
15. *CM,* p. 28.
16. The *Cartesian Meditations* even speak of a *"de facto"* ego (trans.
Cairns, p. 69).
17. As the note of the French translation would seem to do (*Méditations cartésiennes,* trans. Peiffer and Levinas, p. 24).
18. "When I am effecting transcendental reduction and reflecting on
myself, the transcendental ego, I am given to myself *perceptually* as this
ego—in a grasping perception" (*CM,* p. 101).

limit himself to describing what he sees. He does this by means of the sentences and expressions which seem most suggestive to him: words are used by him only to turn us toward the realities we will have to grasp "in themselves." For him, they are never the elements of any construction whatever, not even those of a definition.

In connection with the precise subject we are presently treating, and in trying to place ourselves again in the very movement of phenomenology, it seems to us that any interpretation of the *cogito* which would hold it as a fact must be set aside. We are drawn to this by a remark in the *Ideas*, according to which a science of phenomenological facts could not exist alongside the sciences of ordinary facts.[19]

Facticity, moreover, is characterized by belonging to a nature, that is, by existence in the world. In an even stricter sense, the acts of cognition that found experience, and that thus lie at the origin of the factual sciences, posit a real individual, possessing a spatiotemporal existence.[20] A fact is what is situated and dated and consequently possesses a character of contingency.[21] The very sense of "fact" implies a certain irrationality.

The features of the ego are exactly the opposite: to be sure, the form in accordance with which its contents are organized is time, but the subject remains outside of time while "constituting" its meaning.[22] And even in giving to time the value of an ontological law we limit ourselves to interpreting the consciousness we already have of a world, "of our universally familiar ontological type"; [23] "questions of universal genesis and the genetic structure of the ego in its universality, so far as that structure is more than temporal formation, are still far away" (*ibid.*).

Moreover, the evidence of the "I" is apodictic. The "I" is no longer subject to any contingency. By all these qualities it is thus definitely in contrast to "facts."

Let us not forget that all we can say about the ego occurs

19. *Ideen*, p. 119.
20. *Ibid.*, p. 8.
21. *Ibid.*, p. 9.
22. The ego "constitutes" *all* meanings.
23. *CM*, p. 76.

after the transcendental reduction, that is, when we have placed in brackets, within the world in general, the whole flow of consciousness and our whole psychological life.

It is always difficult to effect the epochē. But what is most painful for us is to reduce our personal psychological life, what we can call our "soul." The transcendental ego is completely different from it, and phenomenology should never be interpreted as a philosophy that would seek reality by basing itself on internal experience, free to push it to a greater "depth." "It is of critical importance for the true sense of transcendental phenomenology to be well assured that *man*, and not only the human body, but also the *human soul*, however purely it may be grasped by internal experience, are only *worldly concepts*." [24] "The psychic life that psychology talks about has in fact always been, and still is, meant as psychic life in the world. Obviously the same is true also of one's own psychic life, which is grasped and considered in *purely internal experience*. . . . By phenomenological epochē I reduce my natural human ego and my psychic life." [25]

The distinction between the transcendental ego and the psychological self is a delicate one to make. But it is at the base of phenomenology, and Husserl continually insists on its importance: the psychological attitude is essentially different from the phenomenological attitude. [26] As early as the *Logical Investigations*, even though he had not yet elucidated the sense of phenomenology, Husserl already knew that it would be something other than psychology. [27] He does not attack introspective psychology as such, but he refuses to confuse phenomenology with a study of internal life, under any form whatever. It is because it did not know how to distinguish the transcendental from the psychological that British empiricism saw itself led toward a subjective idealism full of contradictions, and, for the same reason,

24. *Logik*, p. 223. Italicized in the original.
25. *CM*, pp. 25–26.
26. *Ideen*, p. 104.
27. See, for example, the Introduction to Volume II of the *Logical Investigations*. It is also here that Husserl specifies that his investigations hope to free themselves from all presuppositions, whether metaphysical, physical, or psychological. It is this intention that the phenomenological reduction will later fulfill.

Kant's Copernican revolution was unable to develop all of its consequences.[28]

In Husserl's eyes, "internal perceptions" are of no particular interest; they do not attain true subjectivity: "internal experience is a kind of worldly experience, objective, for the same reason as any other experience of others or any physical experience." [29] We must thus distinguish between "psychological internal experience" and "the evident experience of the *ego cogito*." [30] The *Logical Investigations* even proposed abandoning the classical opposition of external perception and internal perception, which has no importance for the theory of knowledge, taking up instead the opposition of adequate perception and inadequate perception.[31] What preoccupies Husserl is not the greater or lesser "intimacy" of knowledge but the greater or lesser achieved perfection of its evidence. In spite of the frequent use of the term *Erlebnis*—understood, moreover, in different senses in various places—we are dealing with a philosophy of intelligence and not a philosophy of life. Phenomenology is, indeed, itself a life, but it is a "living for truth." [32]

The entire effort made by the phenomenologist in the transcendental reduction thus aims at allowing him to find himself, beyond the world, and consequently beyond psychology and the kinds of experience proper to it. To drive the *cogito* outside psychology is to confirm that it is not a fact. The use Husserl makes of the term "experience" when he talks about the "I think" remains to be explained.

Taken in the strictest sense, experience is nothing other than sensible experience, external or internal—that of the empiricists. Set in opposition to this is the meaning of the *Wesensschau*, the intuition of nonreal essences.[33]

28. *Logik*, p. 226.
29. *Ibid.*, pp. 223–24.
30. *Ibid.*, p. 224.
31. Edmund Husserl, *Log. Unt.*, Part 2 (1st ed.), II, 333. Cf. also all of § VI of the appendix, pp. 708–12.
32. Edmund Husserl, "Krisis," p. 93; *Krisis*, p. 15; *Crisis*, p. 17.
33. *Ideen*, p. 35. Husserl adds here that "this type of act, which gives us things primordially, refers only to the reality of nature; and this act we call experience." He thus defines experience in the strict sense of the term. It is impossible to take the word in the same sense when it concerns the *cogito*, which is outside nature.

But one can also speak of experience in a generalized sense, where the word is employed as having the same sense as the terms "intuition" and "evidence." [34] In this sense it signifies receiving a reality which is given to us "in person." [35] It is then possible to say that eidetic intuition itself is a kind of experience.[36]

These experiences, these intuitions, these evidences (which is to say, these cognitions of objects of thought in accordance with a mode where they are given in person) can be of three different types: they can bear on sensible realities and thus merit the strict title of experience—or on ideal essences—or, finally, on the transcendental ego. These three types of knowledge have in common only the direct way in which the known reality is apprehended. On all other points the difference is complete. The use of the word *experience* is thus not sufficient to authorize us to compare sensible experience to the apprehension of the *cogito* after the phenomenological reduction.

Could we not then liken the knowledge of the transcendental subject to the intuition of an essence? If it is not a fact, could not the *"cogito"* be an idea? Numerous precise texts seem to suggest this.

In the first place, we know that phenomenology is essentially an eidetic investigation.[37] The transcendental ego it attempts to elicit is indeed not an existence but an essence. But essences are obtained by eidetic reduction. The phenomenological reduction would then be only a particular form of eidetic reduction, and

34. "To each fundamental type of objectivity there corresponds . . . a type of *experience*, of *evidence*" (*Logik*, p. 144). ". . . they (experiences bearing on objects that are not real) have the essential property of all experiences or evidences" (*Logik*, p. 145).

35. "Experience is original consciousness" (*CM*, p. 108).

36. "The identity of an ideal and hence its objectivity is to 'be seen' directly (and if we wanted to extend the word to a suitably larger sense: to be directly experienced) . . ." (*Logik*, p. 139).

37. "Pure or transcendental phenomenology will not be premised as *de facto* knowledge but as knowledge of essence (as 'eidetic' knowledge); as knowledge which would exclusively ensure the 'understanding of essences' and of no facts whatsoever" (*Ideen*, p. 4). And again: "As long as it remains pure and does not involve positing the existence of nature, pure phenomenology, considered as a science, can be solely the study of essence and absolutely not the study of existence; and 'self-observation' and any judgment which would be based on such an 'experience' falls outside its domain" ("Phil. als str. Wiss.," p. 318).

transcendental essences would have the same value as the others:
they would only express the structure of a particular "region."

Let us recall how the mind comes to the intuition of essences.
By looking at a thing, by experiencing a fact, whether real or
imaginary, taken as an example, then by arbitrarily varying this
given in imagination, we can have immediate knowledge of the
essence proper to it. The imaginary fact has here the same value
as the real fact, and modifying the object in imagination is the
model procedure for reaching the essence; it prevents our attach-
ing ourselves to purely empirical features. This is what allows
the statement of that apparently paradoxical proposition, that
"*fiction* is the vital element in phenomenology as in all eidetic
sciences." [38]

Do we not come to the "*eidos ego*" in the same way, starting
from the "*de facto ego*" which we find in ourselves and which
plays the role of the exemplar of what is empirically given? [39]
All the multiple new facts offered to us in experiencing the transcendental will first be the object of a description with a certain
empirical character. When we take it up again later, we will be
able, through the eidetic method, to "transfer . . . all empirical
descriptions into a new and fundamental dimension." [40]

To make the phenomenological *cogito* an essence like others
leads us again to make the "I" an experiential datum, since the
essence of the ego is obtained by starting from the empirical ego.
To characterize transcendental phenomenology, it is not enough
to say that it is eidetic. The determination is exact but insufficient;
the essential is constituted by the phenomenological reduction,
by the grasp of oneself *outside the world*—the world in which all
facts, all more or less general, "regional" essences are found. As
soon as we lose sight of the extraworldly character of the "I," we
fall back into nature: this is the gravest and the most constant
danger to which the phenomenologist is exposed. The opposition
of "worldly" and "extraworldly" is the most important distinction
in the whole of phenomenology. All that will be said concerning
the extraworldly must be understood analogically, for, strictly
speaking, nothing in the world exactly corresponds to it. If the

38. *Ideen,* p. 132.
39. *CM,* p. 70.
40. *Ibid.,* p. 69.

Ideas seem to present the phenomenological reduction to us as a transcendental eidetics, it is because they are still situated at the opening stages of the investigation: as we know, only the first volume was published. They retain the naïveté still proper to this degree of the phenomenological attitude, the naïveté which consists in transposing to the transcendental plane the opposition of fact and essence which has meaning only in the world.[41]

Hence the passage from the *de facto ego* to the *eidos ego* is not the path that pure phenomenology actually follows. It is only "to facilitate entrance into phenomenology"[42] that things have first been presented in such a way. In reality transcendental phenomenology bears *immediately* on the essence of the ego. It is eidetic from the first, as the texts referred to above indicate; but it has a quality of perfection which arises from not dealing with model empirical givens, as does ordinary eidetic reduction. It attempts "exploring eidetically the explicit constitution of any transcendental ego whatever . . . ; accordingly all the descriptions and all the problem-determinations treated by us up to now have in fact been translations from the original eidetic form back into that of an empirical description of types."[43]

This passage is particularly enlightening: to facilitate the understanding of phenomenology by readers still entirely involved in the world, the study of the transcendental ego is presented as constituted in a manner analogous to world eidetics, starting from "transcendental facts."[44] Actually, it is nothing of

41. E. Fink, letter of April 18, 1937. [Volumes II and III of the *Ideen* have since been published. See note 38 in the preceding chapter.—Translator.]

42. *CM*, p. 69.

43. *Ibid.*, p. 71.

44. It is perhaps doubtful that the precautions taken by Husserl to bring the reader as far as transcendental subjectivity fulfilled their role. So many succeeding explications, which are later revealed to be imperfect, greatly risk leading—and actually did lead—to misinterpretations of the doctrine. We know that Husserl's first disciples did not follow the later stages of the founder of phenomenology. Some, like Heidegger, claimed to apply the phenomenological method correctly; yet they build philosophies of "involvement," while Husserl wants precisely to "dis-involve" us from the world—free to return there later with an increased effectiveness and a freedom painfully won. Others, taking the means for the end, believed that phenomenology exhausted its concern in the construction of regional ontologies and in applying them to logical and to psychological problems.

the kind. "Transcendental facts" are only translations. Empiricism is definitively eliminated, and we begin to perceive the positive content it is possible to apply to the phenomenological reduction.

The process of ideation, that is, the means of eliciting essences, is not the same in the world and on the transcendental level.[45] Transcendental phenomenology is thus radically distinguished from world eidetics. The latter proceeds from facts to essences. The former goes from any essence whatever to the transcendental subjectivity which is implied by all essences and which constitutes them all. The movement takes place entirely on the level of essences, but the "I think" implied by all the meanings is not absolutely identical with them. At the transcendental level the notion of essence, like that of fact, has only an analogical meaning.[46] The ego is not a means of introducing a new essence *alongside* the others; it posits their common root, the foundation of their value, in short, their principle. The *cogito* is thus, according to an apt formula, "the necessary premise that alone makes possible affirmation, negation, and even doubt." [47]

To summarize: It is impossible to reduce fact to essence or vice versa. It is impossible to resolve the *cogito* into one of these two types of reality. We are in the presence of three different orders which are not, however, separated, since the *cogito* founds both fact and essence. In this way the intention stated by Husserl in the preface to the *Logical Investigations* [48] is realized; here he asked that phenomenology serve as the basis for both psychology, which is a science of facts, and logic, which bears on essences.

Each of these three types of knowledge has its own character, which can be constituted and presented only in intuition. Yet they have a common feature: they are founded on evidence and "in evidence, the thing or the fact is not only indicated in a

---

If this progressive "unveiling" had so little effect, it is because, in our opinion, it corresponds much less to a deliberately chosen process of exposition than to the progressive fashion in which the transcendental realities were revealed to Husserl himself.

45. E. Fink, letter of May 11, 1936.
46. *Ibid.*
47. "Summary of the Classes Given at the Sorbonne on February 23 and 25, 1929," pp. 2–3.
48. (1st ed.), II, 4.

distant and inadequate fashion; it is present to us itself." [49] We can say, then, "our mind reaches the thing itself." [50] In the *Wesensschau* we grasp essences themselves. In sensible perception we apprehend things in an originary manner. So, too, in the *cogito*, which particularly interests us here, the transcendental subject is given to us in person.

The *cogito* is an evidence of the transcendental. To specify its character, we will thus have to provide a twofold series of elucidations: on the one hand, those required by the notion of evidence itself; on the other hand, those demanded by the originary power of the transcendental domain. Let us first examine this second point.

Perception is in some sense immediately and effortlessly available to us; this is why we can see in it, in a way, the fundamental type of the manner in which the known object comes to present itself to us in evidence.[51] Essences must be elicited by eidetic reduction, whose essential mechanism we mentioned above.[52] The transcendental subject is reached by the phenomenological reduction, which shows us how all facts and all meanings necessarily *imply* it.

It has been remarked [53] that the term "implication," which we use here, can lead to equivocation: it can mean "contain" or "require." The second term gives us the correct interpretation here, but without carrying any moral or dynamic quality. The requirement is entirely rational; it is the demand for what we must "suppose," "admit," in order to understand what is in question. The subject is not "contained" in our affirmation or in our experiences, and the phenomenological reduction is neither an abstraction nor an analysis. But the subject is required if our affirmations, whatever they may be, are to have a meaning; this is what the term "necessarily presupposes," used in the *Cartesian Meditations*, quite aptly denotes. It is in this sense that Husserl writes: "Does not rational being assume, even as it does in nature, in order to be actually intelligible, rational theory and a subjec-

49. *Méd. cart.*, p. 9; cf. *CM*, p. 10.
50. *Méd. cart.*, p. 10; cf. *CM*, p. 12.
51. *Logik*, p. 141.
52. See p. 26, above.
53. René Le Senne, *Le Devoir* (Paris, 1930), p. 103.

tivity which accomplishes it?" [54] And again: "Only a radical questioning of the first principles of subjectivity . . . can render objective truth intelligible and reach the ultimate meaning of the existence of the world." [55]

Implication is thus neither an analysis nor a synthesis. It could not be reduced to the effort made to discover an element in observed reality which would be found on the same ontological level. Nor should it cause us to think of a constructive operation of any kind. It is not a matter of completing the perfection of the given by an act of our freedom in order to reach a supreme harmony. The transcendental subject is neither an element belonging to the world, even of the most general kind, nor a cause, even one elevated to metaphysical dignity. It is the extraworldly condition of all meaning.

Nor should it cause us to think of a simple logical subject, which would be only an idea and which, for this reason, would still be in the world, where not only all facts but also all ideas exist.

Within the world there exist implications which the eidetic study must recognize: such and such a determination, by virtue of the sense proper to it, implies another. In this way, each of our cognitions has meaning only in relation to others which it presupposes. Interpreting the return "to the things themselves" as the passive contemplation of givens, each of which is self-sufficient, means attributing to phenomenology the empiricist attitude it has always tried to combat. On the contrary, every cognition stands out clearly against a "background" which it implies and which we have to discover progressively.[56] It always has a certain "horizon," [57] constituted by incompleted intentions and belonging to the core that is actually given, not accidentally but by essence. For example, when I see a chest placed before me, I know there is a bottom and a side I do not see but which *must* exist. You might say they actually could be missing. But then I

54. "Krisis," p. 137; *Krisis*, p. 62; *Crisis*, p. 62.
55. "Krisis," p. 144; *Krisis*, p. 70; *Crisis*, p. 69.
56. Edmund Husserl, manuscript transcribed by Landgrebe, classified in the Husserl Archives as A. VII, 9, pp. 58–61, under the title 'Horizont." This fragment dates from the period 1910–12.
57. *Ibid.* See also *Ideen*, pp. 48 ff.

would have been mistaken, and what I perceived would have had only the *appearance* of a chest. It is of the very essence of such an object to have four lateral sides, a cover, and a bottom, just as it is implied in the very meaning of a sheet of paper whose recto I perceive to have a verso hidden from me. And besides, the very fact that this verso cannot be given to me at the same time as the recto is an essential necessity.

It is especially in perception that such placing into perspective appears as a necessary condition and that the consideration of "horizon" is imposed. In the *Logical Investigations* Husserl sometimes gives the impression that essences can be grasped in isolation.[58] This impression is lessened when one reads the later works. Clear cut in the case of sensible perception,[59] the question is not, however, resolved for essences in an equally categorical manner. Here, we must look to the later constitutive investigations. But what is certain, whatever may be the implications of essences among themselves, is that they all "refer back" to transcendental subjectivity.

How are these implications presented to us? In evidence, which is the final foundation of all knowledge and which, consequently, holds also for the investigation of implications, or, as Husserl sometimes says, for "intentional analysis." [60] We see that we cannot "posit A without positing B"; we see when we ourselves perform the phenomenological reduction that the world implies the transcendental subject. Phenomenology has no need to base its evidence on anything other than oneself: "it is uniquely in seeing that I can draw from seeing what is naturally found there; I must make an intuitive interpretation of the nature proper to such an intuition." [61] The interpretive evidences superimpose themselves, one upon another, *in infinitum*.[62]

We must thus fasten our reflection on the nature and the bearing of evidence. This will lead us to say a few words about

58. We must, however, recognize all that is presented in the Third and Fourth Investigations.
59. No imaginable synthesis can reach complete and perfect adequacy; always it is accompanied by "unfulfilled" pre-intentions and co-intentions (*Méd. cart.*, p. 52; CM, pp. 61–62).
60. CM, pp. 46–49.
61. *Logik*, p. 142.
62. *Ibid*.

the problem of error, which is always a delicate one to pose in a philosophy of intuition. How could an immediate cognition be false?

We are used to connecting the idea of evidence to that of truth. We do so even more naturally in relation to phenomenology, since we are, as we have been told, in a Cartesian atmosphere. Evident ideas should necessarily be true ones. This is what Husserl thinks at the time of the Logical Investigations,[63] and it is still the opinion attributed to him by Hering, despite his familiarity with the Ideas.[64] We think that this is a matter of the naïve confidence proper to the early stages of the investigation. But in the Ideas no ambiguity could remain. On the contrary, the terminology is clearly set: "We need an entirely general term that envelops in its meaning assertoric vision and apodictic intuition." [65] What is most suitable for this is "to choose the word evidence as the most general concept." [66] Thus not all evidences are apodictic. The passage of the Ideas quoted by Hering does not say—as he believes, because he is interpreting it in terms of the Logical Investigations—that all evidence carries with it the certainty of an indubitable truth. It says only that "all intuition which gives us its content primordially [in itself] is a legitimate source of knowledge, that everything presented to us in primordial form in intuition (and so to speak in its concrete and living reality) must be simply accepted as it presents itself, but solely within the limits in which it is given." [67] Bréhier has seen clearly [68] that for phenomenology evidence is not an absolute criterion for truth.

It is rather remarkable that it is when Husserl is the most readily submitting to Cartesian influence that he denounces the classical connection made between the idea of evidence and that of truth. This is perhaps because in Descartes himself the ques-

63. "Evidence . . . which gives luminous certainty, not only to hold-as-true, but to possess the truth itself" (Log. Unt. [1st ed.], I, 111). "Its objective correlative is being in the sense of truth or truth" (ibid., II, 594).
64. Jean Hering, Phénoménologie et philosophie religieuse (Paris, 1926), p. 42.
65. Ideen, p. 285.
66. Ibid., p. 286.
67. Ibid., pp. 43–44.
68. E. Bréhier, Histoire de la philosophie (Paris, 1932), II, 1111.

tion is not resolved in as simple a fashion as is sometimes thought. It is also because Husserl retains from Descartes only the initial attitude of thought, expressed in the first two Meditations, while abandoning the entire metaphysics that Descartes actually constructed. The failure of the Cartesian "system" naturally had to make him more cautious in respect to the method itself: the persistence of error after the discovery of the method shakes the dogmatism of certainty. To explain this, it must be either acknowledged that evidence does not guarantee truth—but then we disavow one of the essential principles of Cartesianism—or recognized that we do not know when we do or do not possess evidence—and this leads us to separate from each other the subjective and objective conditions of truth, which are juxtaposed in the First Rule of the *Method,* yet are essentially different and unable to remain connected unless the undertaking is verified by its success, which is not the case for Descartes's system. Then we have, on one side, clear and distinct ideas, necessarily true, but which are now the object of ideal evidence alone; on the other, our mind, which indeed knows that it must "carefully avoid haste and prejudice" [69] but which no longer possesses any sure sign, any criterion, allowing it to know if doubt has continued long enough, because it never knows if its ideas are completely clear.

Here is a little-studied aspect of Cartesianism: that of knowing how the soul possesses its own ideas. There have been many arguments as to whether clarity and distinctness were sufficient signs of truth and in what case divine veracity had to lend them its guarantee; the relations between the "I think" and the "I am" in the *cogito* have also been studied in all their aspects. The nature of the act in which the "I" grasps its ideas and itself has been less extensively investigated. One of the merits of Husserl's phenomenology is precisely to have felt the importance of the problem and to have sought not to repeat what Descartes said but to make explicit what was latent in his work.[70] Placing the phenomenological reduction at the center of philosophy is precisely the way to show that the *"cogito"* is reached only at the end

69. *Discours de la Méthode*, Part 2, Adam and Tannery, VI, 18.
70. "Krisis," p. 150; *Krisis*, p. 77; *Crisis*, p. 75.

of a special and prolonged effort, without which we could not strictly say that we think.

An analogous problem is posed here in connection with evidence: how does the ego know that its ideas are clear and distinct? Because it knows them immediately? To say that intuition is its own guarantee makes error incomprehensible and conveys a more naïve dogmatism than that of Descartes, who recognizes "that there is still some difficulty in discerning which are those [ideas] we conceive distinctly." [71] Yet, in this case, what need would we have of carefully avoiding haste and prejudice? These precautions are justified only because a chasm is opened, not between truth and our ideas, but between ourselves and our ideas.

We avoid this dualism no better by refusing to separate intelligence from its object in order to see in the idea the act of intelligence itself. The dualism remains because of the very unconsciousness of this act and of our having to take from outside, as a result, as an image, what the act has actually engendered, a condition in which we are never sure of recognizing rightfully the traces of our own activity.

But it is not Cartesianism that is at issue here, and we are speaking of Descartes only to emphasize the difficulty proper to any philosophy of intuition when the recognition of error has made absolute dogmatism untenable. We are now presented with the following alternative: either evidence is related to truth, but we are never sure of possessing evidence—or evidence is the immediate grasp of its object by thought, but ceases to be an absolute guarantee of truth.

We think that Cartesianism must be interpreted in terms of the first of these proposals. Transcendental phenomenology, on the contrary, adheres to the second, although it implies this apparently paradoxical consequence: we can grasp a false reality immediately; [72] truth and existence are separated. Husserl remarks that the conception of evidence which derives truth from a naïve supposition of truth-in-itself is extremely widespread; but

71. *Discours de la Méthode*, Part 4, Adam and Tannery, VI, 33.
72. "The scientist learned long ago that evidence not only has degrees of clarity but that it can also be false evidence" (*Logik*, p. 111).

it remains foreign to phenomenology and does not withstand the profound intentional examination of evident judgments.[73] Truth is not the object of an immediate intuition. It is "the final result of the critique." [74] True judgment is what critical examination confirms to be valid. It is erroneous to see in evidence "an absolute criterion of truth." [75] It is illusory to believe that man possesses such a criterion, which he may apply here or there to his cognitions in order to test their solidity.

Error is not a pure nonbeing. It is a fact that must be accounted for, like all others, by an intentional analysis, that is, by specifying its meaning.[76]

Phenomenology is the enemy of all dogmatism.[77] It shuns any theory of naïve evidence, which would see in it "a kind of signal for consciousness, which would be joined to a judgment . . . and which would cry to us, as a mystical voice coming from another world: here is truth! As if such a voice had something to tell us, we who are free spirits, and had no need to show its credentials of justification!" [78]

Evidence is something else; it is a special mode of the intentional relation connecting the subject to his thoughts. We can be content to "sight" a thing, a fact, a relation. We can also "fill" this empty intention and make the thing itself present to us. This is where we can speak of evidence.[79] It is a "particular modality of positing" an object.[80] It is not the intrusion into consciousness of a reality totally foreign to it. Its correlative is not

73. *Ibid.*, p. 245.
74. *Ibid.*, p. 113.
75. *Ibid.*, p. 140.
76. ". . . of essential necessity and by an intentional analysis, it must be made intelligible how an experience can give in-itself a being as experienced and yet this being can be blocked out (*durchstrichen*)—it must be explained how such an essentially organized experience presents on its horizon other possible experiences which will confirm it—how, on the other hand, it is of its essence to leave open the possibility of experiences which contradict it" (*Logik*, p. 248).
77. "The total ruin of dogmatic metaphysics is the first task to be accomplished in order to found philosophy" (E. Fink, "Die phänom.," p. 339).
78. *Ideen*, p. 300.
79. *CM*, pp. 10, 11, 57.
80. *Ideen*, p. 300.

truth, it is objectivity; [81] but objectivity, like all notions, has a meaning only in and through consciousness.

There are different kinds of evidence. They can first be classified according to the domain in which they are active. This is what we did earlier.[82] They can also be distinguished according to their modalities: the evidence of a perception, which is perhaps the primitive form of evidence, simple and direct, is something different from the evidence of a memory.[83] But what is more important is to distinguish evidences according to their degree of perfection, according to their greater or lesser adequacy. In imperfect evidence the experience is "vitiated by the *components of a signifying intention which are not yet fulfilled by a corresponding intuition.*" [84] The perfect experience, which would no longer include any intention of meaning left unfulfilled, would merit the designation "adequate evidence." Perhaps it must be located "in infinity." [85] In any case, eidetic analysis shows us that we could not possess it on the level of sensible evidence: it is the very essence of the thing to always appear to us partially. Perception is necessarily inadequate.[86]

Finally, we can judge evidences, no longer according to their character of being more or less adequate, but according to the guarantees of certainty they offer. From this point of view their perfection will be in their apodicticity, that is, in their excluding "in advance every doubt as objectless, empty." [87] We will then have to notice that, in evidence, adequacy and apodicticity need not go hand in hand.[88] Particularly in the experience of the *cogito,* which is of special interest to us here, we find ourselves confronting apodictic evidence; it is, to be sure, the only one possessing such perfection, but neither can this be denied it. One can deny the apodicticity of the "I am" only if, "instead of rendering this [apodicticity] present, one confines oneself to arguing in an

81. *Logik,* p. 144.
82. P. 57, above.
83. *Logik,* p. 141.
84. *Méd. cart.,* p. 13; cf. *CM,* pp. 14–15. (Italics in the original.)
85. *CM,* p. 15.
86. *Ideen,* p. 286; *CM,* p. 61.
87. *CM,* p. 16.
88. *CM,* p. 22.

entirely external manner." [89] This evidence of the *ego cogito*, which is not solely its immediate cognition, which we could later doubt, as we can do where it is a question of empirical cognition, but which is the absolute inconceivability of its negation, is, however, far from adequate. We cannot doubt that we think, but the "core" of adequate experience presented to us in this experience is very sparse: it is nothing more than "the ego's living presence (which the grammatical sense of the sentence, *ego cogito*, expresses)." [90]

We would hope to have given the sense of how much rationality, of how much care, indeed, of how much positive content there is in the steps performed by phenomenology in arriving at the *cogito*. There is nothing dogmatic or naïve in the intuitionism upon which it is based: on the contrary, we find everywhere the constant desire to elucidate the meaning of the propositions asserted and to measure as precisely as possible their authentic value. It remains to be seen what we have won by this approach. Descartes has seldom been challenged on the certainty of his *cogito*. All that he wished to deduce from it has been less easily accepted. Is it not the same for phenomenology? Does not our demand for certainty leave us confronting such a thin, feeble content that it will be of neither interest nor importance to us? How can the radical return to the pure *ego cogito* enable us to revive eternal values and to construct a philosophy? We will try to give a very general idea of this in the next chapter.

89. *Méd. cart.*, p. 19; cf. *CM*, p. 22.
90. *CM*, pp. 22–23.

5 / The Life Proper to the Transcendental Ego

I THINK. This is a truth—perhaps the only one—which it is impossible for me to doubt. Its evidence is apodictic, but it is far from adequate;[1] that is, it is far from giving us a system of perfectly distinct ideas, offering themselves clearly to us. Recognizing the *cogito*, far from providing us complete satisfaction, reveals a new task imposed upon us, about which we could previously have no idea: by a series of entirely new steps we must make this "I think" explicit. The *cogito* could not actually be, as Descartes seems to have thought, a truth which would be located on the same level as scientific and metaphysical propositions and which alone would possess absolute certainty, permitting it to be a solidly established point of departure. Descartes maintains that being is a univocal notion; he says "I am," "God is," "the world is." We must recognize, however, if we are true to the principle of pure intuition, that the *cogito* introduces us into an "infinite realm of being of a new kind."[2] We will thus have to seek what the being of the world signifies and correlatively what the existence of the transcendental ego signifies.

I think, and I am sure that I think; but what does it mean "to think"? At the beginning of the Third Meditation, Descartes answers this question by an empirical enumeration: "I am a thinking being, that is, a being that doubts, asserts, denies, under-

1. *CM*, pp. 22–23.
2. *Ibid.*, p. 27.

[71]

stands a few things, is ignorant of many, loves, hates, is willing or unwilling, that also imagines and feels." [3] But this leaves unexplained what it is that joins all these aspects in the unity of thought. It also risks falling back, in the course of a description which is not sufficiently methodical, from the transcendental ego —whose necessity we have recognized—to the psychological subject, whose features we could undoubtedly describe but which is in the world and for this very reason ceases to be apodictic. It is only analogically that we will be able to state our task: *"the realm accessible to transcendental self-experience* . . . must be explored" [4] and its modalities described. These are formulas forced upon us by the necessity of expressing in *worldly* language what is beyond the world. The *transcendental* is not set against the *world* as two regions which would be distinguished at the center of being: it has a manner of being proper to itself.[5] Any description of consciousness is thus in constant danger of making us descend to the psychological level, that is, to nature. The recognition of creative freedom, of the power to do or not to do, would not be sufficient to truly raise us above nature: it would still be only a nature, but an irrational one.

We must rid ourselves of the persistent illusion according to which the phenomenologist, once situated in the transcendental *dimension*, would behave analogously to a psychologist or a scientist acting in the world. We know that "this self and its psychic life, which I necessarily retain in spite of the epochē, are not part of the world." [6] Yet phenomenology does not turn away from the world. It does not claim to reveal to us *another* world, which would be self-sufficient and whose description it would give. The ego's life transcends the world, not because it is foreign to the world, but because it *constitutes* the world. Let us recall that "the name of the problem which inspires all of phenomenology is intentionality." [7] Consciousness is not a substance whose accidents would be feelings and ideas, and thinking is not simply

3. *Third Meditation*, Adam and Tannery, IX, 27.
4. *CM*, p. 29.
5. E. Fink, "Die phänom.," p. 369.
6. *Méd. cart.*, p. 21; cf. *CM*, p. 25.
7. Edmund Husserl, *Ideen*, p. 303.

unraveling successive episodes of an internal dream. Thought has a bearing on things. Its own nature is such that it never closes in upon itself but goes outside itself to rush *toward* its objects; it is a thought of something. "In each actual *cogito* a *regard,* radiating from a pure I, is directed toward the *object* of each correlative of consciousness, toward the thing, the relation, etc." [8]

Being an ego, and being aware of being an ego, does not mean, then, cutting oneself off from the world and turning in on oneself in order to better feel the ineffable nuances of this personal intimacy. It does not even mean grasping a pure "I think." Here the adequate formula is *"ego—cogito—cogitatum,"* [9] for "the transcendental ego . . . is what it is solely in relation to intentional objects." [10] The task presented to phenomenology when, by reason of the *cogito,* it has become conscious of itself, is to explain "the origin of the world." [11] The phenomenological reduction showed us that we had to look for it in transcendental subjectivity: all facts in the world, all essences, send us back to the transcendental ego as the ultimate term which alone appears to us as necessary. There is no need, then, to founder in the irrational; rather we must come back to the world to understand it in terms of the mind.[12] Describing the life of the ego is seeing how it constitutes its *cogitatum.*

The two fundamental ideas of phenomenology are the phenomenological reduction and the theory of constitution.[13] The first allows the mind to discover its own nature and to elicit from it the forms under which it appears to itself in the world as a determined being, as man.[14] Through it the mind, which had been lost in nature, finds itself and frees itself. Then and only then does it become capable of beginning a new task: interpreting the world as a coherent system constituted by the mind.

All the elements of the world—of this radically insufficient world—refer back to the unity of the I which is a guarantee of

8. *Ibid.,* pp. 168–69.
9. *CM,* p. 50.
10. *Ibid.,* p. 65 (modified); cf. *Méd. cart.,* p. 55.
11. E. Fink, "Die phänom.," p. 344.
12. E. Fink, "Was will . . . ," p. 31.
13. E. Fink, "Die phänom.," p. 344.
14. E. Fink, "Was will . . . ," p. 28.

the coherence of the world. But this is only a general affirmation of the whole. Is the relation of the I to its *cogitata* simple and always similar? This cannot be asserted a priori. The development of the constitutive investigations, always made following the same intuitive method, will show, on the contrary, that there are different forms of intentionality, that is, diverse ways for the ego to constitute its object.

Let us try to specify the sense Husserl gives to this term "constitution." First, we can say that it designates the original relation of the I to the world, as a whole, and of the I to each of the structures which are delineated in the world, in their particularity. These are the aspects of the world whose *sense*, which would lead us to the transcendental ego, we have sought to understand. To grasp the constitution of the world by the ego will then be a matter of seeing how the I gives a *sense* [15] to everything presented to us in the world and how, in particular, it gives an existential sense, a value of being, to certain aspects of this world. We must place ourselves on the level of meaning in order to accurately understand the theory of constitution. But, in a more general sense, it seems this is always advisable in order to understand phenomenology. The *Logical Investigations* have already encouraged us to do this. And more recent works more clearly confirm it. Phenomenology does not seek self-experience but self-understanding (*Selbstverständigung*).[16] "The world itself has its being in its entirety only as a certain *sense*, which supposes absolute consciousness, as the origin of meanings" (*Feld der Sinngebung*).[17] Phenomenological idealism does not deny the true existence of the world.[18] Its sole task is to elucidate the *sense* of this world. It is beyond doubt that the world exists. But this indubitability must be understood.

The transcendental subject itself does not escape this general rule. It is not a being we would grasp directly, outside of any phenomenal deformation. This is not a "given" which is more solid than the others, a "primitive fact" of which we would be unable

15. Edmund Husserl, "Nachwort," p. 550.
16. *Ibid.*, p. 557.
17. *Ideen*, p. 107.
18. On this point see p. 107, below; see also the beginning pages of Chapter 3.

to rid ourselves. It is only what possesses "the existential sense of absolute being." [19] The *Cartesian Meditations* also speak of the world "as a constituted sense," [20] of the "world as a unity of sense." [21] But the transcendental ego knows itself; we must say even that it "exists for itself in continuous evidence." [22] As such it also will itself be a certain sense, and we will see arising the constitutive problems of the transcendental ego itself.[23] Transcendental idealism actually wants to do nothing other than to clarify the "*sense* of every kind of being that I, the *ego*, can imagine." [24]

But the dogmatism proper to those who retain "the natural attitude" prevents them from understanding a philosophy which places itself entirely in the perspective of meaning. It is not a question here of giving a primary importance to *sense* but of no longer conceiving problems other than those of meaning. Hence, we must cease—and this is not easy—implicitly presupposing under meanings "things" capable of supporting them and which consciousness would later make intelligible by applying to them its own form. This conception is of Kantian inspiration. Several interpreters of phenomenology thought it was found in Husserl and saw therein evidence that the father of phenomenology was returning to the positions of critical philosophy. But transcendental subjectivity does not confer a sense upon a pre-existing thing. Phenomenology does not accept the thing-in-itself: "experience is not an opening in a kind of conscious space, through which there appears a world existing prior to all experience; nor is it simply receiving into consciousness something foreign to consciousness." [25] Thus sense is not imposed upon a prior material which would later be given form. Phenomenology does not recognize the dualism of matter and form, or at least does not view it in an irreducible and absolute manner. It is in an entirely relative way that an "intentional sense" and a "hyletic matter" can be distinguished. These concepts do not correspond to the

19. "Nachwort," p. 562.
20. *CM*, p. 137.
21. *Méd. cart.*, p. 23; cf. *CM*, p. 26.
22. *Méd. cart.*, p. 55; cf. *CM*, p. 66.
23. *CM*, p. 66.
24. *Méd. cart.*, p. 72; cf. *CM*, p. 86.
25. Edmund Husserl, *Logik*, p. 206.

Kantian oppositions they might bring to mind.[26] Matter is itself constituted.[27]

But into what ghostly world have we fallen? What is a system of meanings unsupported by anything? Can we speak of meanings if there are no beings to "receive" this or that sense? Granted, in logic we put the metaphysical domain out of bounds. But to concretely set up a knowledge cut off from being, an "abstract" knowledge, isn't this a flagrant contradiction?

It seems to us one could not triumph by simple objections of this kind. Phenomenology requires that we assume a new attitude. It in no way resembles a kind of purely intellectual dialectic. It is a movement of being as a whole. It does not seek, then, to oppose its reasons to those of realism or to make use of those by which idealism has enriched the history of philosophy. We must laboriously, patiently, make the effort of detachment and liberation included in the term "phenomenological reduction" in order to "see" that we have not discarded the concrete in discarding realism.[28] We do not lose being by being exclusively interested in meanings, because the field of meaning is more vast than that of being. To have a "sense" is not a certain manner of being. It is being, on the contrary, which is a certain meaning. It no longer appears as the general and absolute background against which everything stands out. It is a sense, an idea.[29] Far from narrowing our perspective, we widen it instead by passing from a philosophy of being to a transcendental phenomenology, since the latter allows us to understand the former by building a theory of the constitution of being. In transcending realism, phenomenology does not abandon ontology, and all eidetic analyses effected before the phenomenological reduction will keep their value. If transcendental philosophy goes beyond ontology, it is not to destroy it but to found it. Hence it can itself assume the title of concrete ontology and present itself as a "concrete logic of being." [30]

26. E. Fink, "Die phänom.," p. 375.
27. Ibid., p. 376.
28. On this point see, for example, § 55 of the Ideen, pp. 106–8.
29. ". . . 'the existent' is a practical idea, that of the infinity of theoretically determining work" (CM, p. 88).
30. CM, p. 155.

Thus, constitution is not only "informative"; it is truly creative.

How must this creation be understood? The terms that express it are rather diverse. Here again, driven by his desire rather to suggest to us a direction to explore than to construct a theory with words, Husserl seems to have been little concerned about unifying his vocabulary. In certain places Husserl speaks of "productive action" (*das Ich . . . schafft produktiv*).[31] In the *Logic*, creative construction is likened to an "active realization" (*aktive Erfüllung*).[32] Objectivizing constitution is even presented to us [33] as a kind of unconscious activity which makes (*macht*), which operates in a thematic manner. We do not believe that these expressions should be taken literally. The transcendental subject does not "make" anything, strictly speaking. All action unfolds in the world; it is, consequently, a constituted structure. It is here in particular that we must recall the inevitable deformation that language imposes on transcendental concepts: "Every phenomenological discourse sees its sense completely transformed to the very extent that it employs natural language." [34]

Other texts, moreover, warn us that phenomenology wants neither to deduce anything [35] nor to construct anything.[36] The investigations of a constitutive nature are not those which would attempt to give us the secret of some magical operation, whether conscious or not; they are simply those by which "we inquire into the universal types of possible modes of consciousness of objects." [37] Is it a question of particular constitutive theories? Husserl tells us that "it is everywhere a matter of uncovering the intentionality implicit in the experience itself as a transcendental process." [38]

It seems possible to us to resolve these uncertainties only if

31. Edmund Husserl, manuscript transcribed by Landgrebe, p. 23, classified in the Husserl Archives as A, V, 10, under the general heading *Zur Beschreibung der Umwelt*.
32. *Logik*, p. 160.
33. *Ibid.*, p. 30.
34. Edmund Husserl, manuscript transcribed by Landgrebe, A, V, 10, p. 23.
35. "Nachwort," p. 553.
36. *Ibid.*, p. 552.
37. *CM*, p. 53.
38. *Ibid.*, p. 64.

we return to the fundamental phenomenological distinction, that of the transcendental and the worldly: constitution can be expressed in worldly terms only analogically; it is, indeed, a relation between the I who is outside the world and the world taken as a whole—the world which includes what we call transcendent as well as what we call immanent and which envelops nonbeing as it does being. Constitution is a relation which is "neither receptive nor productive." [39]

Thus we will avoid—as far as possible—terms which would suggest either the passivity or the activity of the subject. To translate the term *Leistung*, which Husserl employs quite frequently in connection with the "life proper" to the transcendental ego, the least dangerous word would perhaps be *act*, which Husserl himself uses readily (*Akt*), and which philosophical tradition is not in the habit of confusing with *action*. This conjunction can be justified by the fact that, taken in its widest sense, the Husserlian *act* (*Akt*) expresses nothing other than intentionality itself,[40] that is, the relation to the object. But the acts of the I (*Leistungen*) also designate this relation, by emphasizing simply that it rightly constitutes the object, obviously excluding any idea of "manufacturing." To translate *leisten* we will use the verb "accomplish" as the one which least risks making us think of such manufacturing.

We believe one must refuse both the interpretations which would delineate constitution in the sense of activity and those

39. E. Fink, "Die phänom.," p. 373.
40. Edmund Husserl, *Log. Unt.* (1st ed.), p. 388. The definition of act [*Akt*] remains the same in the second edition (Vol. II, part 1, p. 413), with, however, a difference in the way in which the knowledge of this relation to the object is represented to us. The 1901 edition makes it a property one can live, experience (*erlebbare Eigenthümlichkeit*). The 1913 edition sees it as "a property belonging to the essential constitution proper to the experience of act." Concerning the sense of act, see also *Ideen*, pp. 64 and 170. Here, Husserl distinguishes from act in a broad sense, act in a narrower, more precise sense, which will signify only *actual*, completed acts. Charles Serrus can thus define act precisely as being "the effectuation of a signification in a sense" (*Etudes philosophiques*, IV, No. 2 [1930], 127). This restricted sense sees its importance diminished, however, as Husserl has less and less confidence in the possibility of adequate effectuations and as he insists more on the imperfect character of all we apprehend (or almost all), always surrounded by a *horizon* of intentions not effected.

which would compare it to some sort of passivity. Constitution is not an event which would occur somewhere, even beyond the world, in a kind of "metaphysical space." [41] The problem of constitution indicates nothing other than the possibility "of examining intuitively and grasping theoretically" the series of fixed phenomena which are joined in the unity of an object; [42] these series will be able to be "analyzed and described in their eidetic uniqueness." [43]

In the *cogito* as in constitution—which is only the expansion and the differentiation of the *cogito*—the self is neither active nor passive. Constitution is indeed creative, since there was nothing before it. But the relation to the object is a relation of knowledge, an intuition. This does not mean that the I confronts the world as an indifferent spectator, totally foreign to the spectacle presented to it. This would again mean representing, in space, relations which are beyond space, as they are beyond all natural symbols by which we seek to make them present for us. We must learn to unite concepts we are in the habit of opposing: phenomenology is a philosophy of *creative intuition*. The intellectual vision really creates its object—not the semblance, the copy, the image of the object, but the object itself. It is evidence, this completed form of intentionality, which is constitutive.

Husserl's intellectualism, or, more precisely, the superiority he accords to theoretical thought, confirms that it is indeed intuition that posits the object.

Phenomenology is not narrow because it does not proceed from an unjustified initial assertion which would later have to be saved by any means. The fundamental value given to intuition expresses nothing other than this docility in regard to the real, this freedom from prejudgments (*absolute Voraussetzungslosigkeit*).[44] Thus, Husserl has no difficulty in recognizing what is original in the acts of consciousness which are not theoretical: the *positing* of a feeling, a duty, a value of whatever sort, must be studied by respecting the particular features, not only of the ob-

41. E. Fink, "Was will . . . ," p. 30.
42. *Ideen*, p. 315.
43. *Ibid.*, p. 316.
44. Cf. *Log. Unt.* (2d ed.), II, Part 1, Introduction, § 7, pp. 19–22. Cf. also Edmund Husserl, "Phil. als str. Wiss.," p. 341.

ject being posited, but also of the transcendental act by which it is constituted. Moral life, aesthetic life, emotional life will thus have their peculiar nature respected. Husserl even goes so far as to say that each of these *regions* of existence will have to have its own constitutive phenomenology.[45]

However, all these "positings," all these "acts," do not have the same importance. Some can be missing without any contradiction and without the complete disappearance of the object posited. Its theoretical positing, on the contrary, or, more precisely, to use Husserl's vocabulary, the "doxic thesis," [46] can never be missing.

If, for example, we consider a moral judgment, we notice that its object is posited in several ways at the same time. On the one hand, to be sure, it is posited as an original *moral* given: it is when we concretely live the life of duty that morality is really known to us. In a general manner, we can say that value is presented to consciousness only in the concrete experience of the evaluation.[47] At the same time, the moral object will be able to be the object of aesthetic or affective appreciation. But it is especially the specifically moral "positing" that will always be accompanied by a doxic "positing": this task offered to my will, whose awesomeness excites my admiration but whose difficulty staggers me, is the idea of a certain series of acts which are doubtless not real but which, precisely, must be made real. Duty does not abstract from reality; it simply presents it according to its own mode.

Thus in moral consciousness the transcendental act is *polythetic*. There is rightly an affective or a moral positing because there is an affective or moral intentionality. But these exist only as accompanied by doxic positing, that is, by existential belief in one or another of its modes, yet always preserving its properly theoretical character.

45. *Ideen*, p. 319.
46. For Husserl *doxa* has the sense of belief (*Glauben*). It must be interpreted more in terms of Hume's *Belief* than of Plato's *doxa*. The "doxic thesis" is then one which introduces the object as really existing, which makes us believe in its reality (actual or potential). This is what gives thought its seriousness. It is not necessary to recall that for Husserl this belief has in no way the character of a fiction.
47. *Ideen*, p. 243.

Doubtless it is not necessary that I be attentive to the theoretical aspect of my representation; thus the objectivity of what causes my embarrassment or my enthusiasm can be—and often is—purely potential. But the theoretical aspect implicitly remains. It must always be there, for it alone will permit evaluations to develop their proper sense. The act posits its object, "but whatever be the quality of its positing, it also posits it in a doxic manner; what is posited by this act in other modes is also posited as being; only, not [as] actual being." [48] "The doxic *cogito* alone realizes an actual objectification." [49] This is what founds the universality of logic, since "each act or each correlative of an act conceals within itself an explicit or implicit aspect." [50]

Levinas, a commentator who deeply penetrates Husserl's thought, clearly shows "the primacy of theoretical consciousness in the constitution of being." [51] But he seems to us to betray the spirit of the doctrine by seeing here only a kind of narrowness in phenomenology, which had not yet been "separated from the theory of knowledge." [52] It is not extending Husserl's philosophy to separate out, "in sometimes going beyond a strict interpretation," [53] "the elements of his doctrine which seem to us to lead toward a richer notion of existence than presence before a contemplating consciousness." [54] It means opposing the central idea of the system. It is to refuse the supreme evidence toward which the phenomenological reduction leads us. The "I" does not confront a reality to be contemplated. Being arises from its very regard. What, seen from the side of the subject (noetically), is belief, is, seen from the side of the object (noematically), existence.[55] It is the error of dogmatism to set one against the other, mind against things, thus creating the illusory and insoluble problem of their communication. This will then be conceived as a transitive relation analogous to those we grasp in nature—for

48. *Ibid.*
49. *Ibid.*, p. 244.
50. *Ibid.*
51. E. Levinas, *La Théorie de l'intuition dans la phénoménologie de Husserl* (Paris, 1930), p. 192.
52. *Ibid.*
53. *Ibid.*
54. *Ibid.*
55. *Ideen*, p. 215.

dogmatism is only another name for naturalism. The difference between idealism and realism will consist solely in that, for the latter, being engenders belief, while, for the former, belief creates the fiction of being. But, for transcendental phenomenology, the "I" no more constructs objects than it suffers them. It is beyond action and passion.

Hence when we pass from polythetic to monothetic acts, this in no way means that we accord an unjustified privilege to one of the traditionally natural faculties of man, as Levinas seems to think,[56] but only that we separate the essential form of intentionality, which posits the object in general, from accidental forms which posit certain ways of being of the object: the object as lovable, as hatable, etc. Husserl does not place intelligence above emotion. He situates within the field of meaning in general the particular meanings of emotion, moral law, etc.

Nor is phenomenology an incomplete philosophy, which would have neither the strength nor the courage to go beyond the theory of knowledge. A theory of knowledge seeks the value and limits of knowledge. It thus conceals a latent dogmatism incompatible with the spirit of phenomenology. For the latter, knowledge can have no limits, and there is nothing outside it which could give it external justification. There is no radical unintelligible: the theory of constitution basically asserts only the indefinite possibility of analyzing and describing the series of phenomena and their systematic grouping, understanding them completely and "stripping them of any enigma."[57] The absurd is itself a certain meaning, which is brought out in the phenomenology of evidence,[58] and *"reason is not an accidental de facto ability . . .* but rather a title for an *all-embracing essentially necessary structural form belonging to all transcendental subjectivity."*[59]

The phenomenological reduction cannot be defined from outside in any adequate manner: it must be effected in order for its true nature to be understood. It is the same for the theory of constitution. It cannot be expressed in worldly terms, since it is the

56. Levinas, *La Théorie de l'int.*, p. 193.
57. *Ideen*, p. 316.
58. *Ibid.*, p. 300.
59. *CM*, p. 57.

theory of the origin of the world. It is only by entering into the detail of constitutive investigations that it will be possible to penetrate its meaning.[60]

Husserl's published work does not develop these constitutive analyses, which do, however, hold an important place in his manuscripts. We find there only general indications, allusions, and, in short, a simple outline of studies. The *Ideas* speak only briefly of constitution; yet they sketch the outline of certain constitutive studies, for example, those bearing on the constitution of the "thing," which are particularly important, as Husserl took the region "thing" as "the transcendental guideline." [61] We find other sketches of constitutive analyses in the *Cartesian Meditations*, in connection with the self, the concrete monad, and the personality of others.

Here we encounter a difficulty which we have doubtless had during the entire course of our study but which is greater now that it is a question of the problems of elucidation which Husserl was working on when he died. It concerns the very way Husserl worked, his indifference to success, his taste for concrete work, the nature of his mind, less attracted by the exposition of knowledge gained, and even less by justifying results in view of criticism, than by the discovery of new truths. As Landgrebe justly writes, "He wanted only one thing: to receive the light"; [62] and he preferred to reserve for study the time that would have otherwise been consumed by distinguishing concepts and by polemics. So, pushed by this prospective energy, he speaks in his books of what must yet be done rather than of what he has already accomplished. His published works are mostly devoted to the work of clearing away, necessary before any study, and to presenting

60. See, for example, E. Fink, "Die phänom.," p. 373.

61. *Ideen*, p. 313. This exemplary character of the constitution of things does not avoid disturbing somewhat the comprehension of phenomenology. We actually risk assimilating to the thing regions of being which are quite different from it or, which is even more serious, transcendental subjectivity itself. Fink insists on the fact that the process of ideation is quite different according to whether it is a question of the ontic sphere (that is, the world) or the transcendental sphere.

62. L. Landgrebe and J. Patocka, "Edmund Husserl zum Gedächtnis," *Schriften des Prager Philosophischen Cercles* (Prague: Academia Verlagsbuchhandlung, 1938), p. 11.

the program to be completed. Concrete investigations have indeed been effected, but they have not been published; and the manuscripts containing them are practically unusable in their present state.[63] In any case, a general theory of constitution would not be found there which, once the constitutive analyses were effected, would return to the question of constitution in order to elicit its sense, range, and exact nature.

For lack of such a "phenomenology of phenomenology," we will content ourselves with utilizing the general indications found in the *Ideen,* the *Logic,* or the *Cartesian Meditations* and with seeing how Husserl approaches the constitutive analyses found there.

Let us first note that constitution has a universal character: everything is constituted; not only the "thing" spoken about in sections 150 and 151 of the *Ideen,* but all the regions of the object [64] or, more precisely, of the world.[65] The man I am is constituted, as is the animal, as are intersubjective realities, values, social orders, and cultural ideals.[66] Nor are the most general forms of consciousness, space and time, given to the mind as realities to be taken as they are and which would themselves be inexplicable: they have their own constitution, proper to them.[67]

---

63. Among other causes, this comes from their having been written in shorthand and their containing signs and abbreviations peculiar to Husserl. Only those disciples very familiar with Husserl's thought and his work habits could restore them to "clarity."

64. *Ideen,* p. 318.

65. In the precise sense of the term, the object for Husserl is the intentional object, the identical end to which the multiple states of consciousness refer (*Ideen,* pp. 187, 189, 205, 207).

66. *Ideen,* p. 318.

67. A work on *Time Constitution* was to have appeared in 1938 under the dual authorship of Edmund Husserl and Eugen Fink. Husserl's death obviously made its publication impossible in that form. A reworking which will separate the passages edited by Husserl himself from those written by Fink is necessary. [A number of manuscripts written between 1915 and 1925 dealing with time constitution were given to Fink by Husserl for transcription and reworking. They formed the second group of writings on time constitution, the first having been those included in the volume published with Heidegger, *Zeitbewusstseins,* and the third group, those manuscripts written during the period Husserl worked on *Krisis.* The writings referred to by Berger have never been published, although section C of the Husserl Archives (*Zeitkonstitution als formale Konstitution*) contains

In addition: the ego constitutes itself as existing, since "the ego exists for itself in continuous evidence." [68] "The other" is also a constituted reality, not only as a state or moment of my own life of consciousness, but really as the other and precisely as something *other*.[69] There will also be a constitutive theory of the body proper, as there will be one of the earth, of "our" earth. Finally, and what appears most antagonistic to any expository theory, *fact* in its very opacity and in its historicity is still—just like nothingness or the absurd—a constituted reality.[70]

But what does Husserl do in these constitutive analyses? Is it a matter for him of *manufacturing* the world or at least of *shaping* it? We have already rejected this interpretation.[71] Examining the concrete steps of constitution will permit us, we think, to reinforce our interpretation of constitution understood as a creation by intuition.[72] Husserl does nothing other than elicit what is implied by the *sense* of the region he is studying: What does it mean to have one's own body? What does it mean to be an "alter ego"? What are presupposed in terms of elements not given but which must, however, be admitted under penalty of stripping what is studied of all meaning?

Let us return, for example, to the constitution of the thing as it is presented to us in the *Ideen*.

The phenomenologist takes as a "guideline" a certain region

---

the writings on time constitution which have been transcribed to date.—Translator.]

68. *Méd. cart.*, p. 55; cf. *CM*, p. 66.

69. *Ibid.*, p. 94.

70. We cannot help comparing the Husserlian conception of "fact" to the notion of "shock," as presented by Brunschvicg in *Modalité du jugement* (pp. 92, 94, 100, 115). To be sure, for Brunschvicg the nature of shock would be precisely not to be constituted, to be what is in opposition to perfect intelligibility. But the external relation necessarily possesses, as relation, a certain *sense*, and it is precisely this *sense* that Husserl retains in order to *constitute* the fact. The fact of being given, historicity, is not for Husserl, as for dogmatic idealism, an illusion to be dissipated, but particular meanings to be elucidated: it is the *sense of the fact* to offer opposition to the mind.

71. See in particular pp. 77 ff., above.

72. A text in the *Logic* presents explicitly the theory of creative intuition. Husserl notes there that "the phenomenological a priori . . . (is) . . . created by the corresponding eidetic intuitions, as such a source is generally implicit in the sense of phenomenology" (*Logik*, p. 218).

of the world, in this case the region "material thing," and he is going to seek the transcendental acts to which its features correspond.

All regional essences refer back to transcendental consciousness, but each region must, in addition, refer back to a particular modality of the life of the "I." By intuitively studying the concrete cases as examples (whether real or imaginary) according to the eidetic method, we will arrive at the essence of the thing. But, enlightened by the phenomenological reduction concerning the necessary relation to the subject, to the ego, we will notice that even if this essence can be given to us immediately, *originaliter*, it is, however, necessarily inadequate. At least it conceals in itself a rule specifying in what way it can be completed indefinitely,[73] in determined directions, which will vary only with each particular type of thing. To form the constitutive theory of things will consist simply in recognizing these necessary directions according to which phenomena can indefinitely be evoked, all converging, intentionally, on the same center. The idea of a thing will thus be progressively elucidated, constitution acting as well through superimposed levels: first, the simple *res extensa*, then the thing as substantive reality involved in relations of causality,[74] and, finally, the thing as an identical object valid for different subjects.[75]

This initial sketch of a constitutive theory is still vague. It scarcely goes beyond objective eidetic analyses except for the mention—on the whole, merely rhetorical—of a noetic aspect, the correlative of the noematic aspect of the thing.[76]

The *Cartesian Meditations* offer us extremely condensed texts but allow us, nevertheless, to form a more precise idea of constitution: actually, the object of the study receives its proper

73. *Ideen*, pp. 314, 315, 316.
74. *Ibid.*, p. 316.
75. *Ibid.*, p. 317.
76. These very indications are dangerous to phenomenology; it risks being improperly compared to Kantianism, to the extent that we are led to believe that the noetic act "would construct" its noema by an indefinitely continued synthesis. In his article in *Kantstudien* (p. 374), Fink justly notes the confusions made possible by the elliptical and somewhat preparatory passages of the *Ideen*. On the meaning of synthesis in Husserl's philosophy, see p. 93.

sense only through transcendental subjectivity and, in some sense, as a modality of the *cogito*. We do not always go outside meaning to reach being. In the eyes of the phenomenologist, such a procedure makes no sense: it is naïve metaphysics, which deals with "absurd things in themselves." [77] But we are aware that the sense of regional objects was still imperfectly elucidated as long as we did not discover to what phases of the life of thought the structures corresponded. It is no longer a question of receiving an essence as a crude and somewhat irrational given but of "how, in itself and by virtue of its current intentional structure, consciousness makes possible and necessary the fact that such an 'existing' and 'thus determined' Object is intended in it, occurs in it as such a sense." [78]

It is the "same object" which will be posited by consciousness as present, as evoked by memory or formed by imagination; as real or illusory; as belonging to me or as foreign. Here implication, some ideas implying others, is insufficient: "sense" has its origin in the attitude of the ego. The simple "material thing" mentioned in the *Ideas* does not itself have its unity in itself, and we can understand its true meaning only by making present in intuition one of the fundamental features of consciousness, which is to *go beyond* "at any moment what is referred to at that moment 'explicitly.'" [79] This is what imprints its own mark on intentional analysis: it is not the carving-out of a given, but "reaches out beyond the particular objects that are to be analyzed": [80] all intentionality implies a horizon.

Equipped with this new method, we will first study the constitution of an intentional object in general and then that of each type of object by eliciting its noetic-noematic structure, especially by interpreting it and systematically explicating it "in respect to those modes of intentional flux that pertain to it, and in respect to their horizons and the intentional processes implicit in their horizons, and so forth." [81] To study the constitution of an object, of a *cogitatum*, then, if we are to understand it fully, to reach in

77. *CM*, p. 156.
78. *Ibid.*, p. 47.
79. *Méd. cart.*, p. 40; cf. *CM*, p. 46.
80. *Méd. cart.*, p. 41; cf. *CM*, p. 48.
81. *CM*, p. 51.

relation to it the perfect rationality that Husserl always sought, is to see to what intention of the transcendental ego it corresponds, see how its manifest aspects and its potential horizons were implied by the very nature of this intention.

We have neither the desire nor the opportunity to consider here, by commenting on them, the constitutive investigations of the *Cartesian Meditations.* Let us simply isolate some aspects, less to gain results than to see a method in action.

One of the most important moments of transcendental phenomenology is its response to the objection of solipsism.[82] How is Husserl going to answer this objection? By a series of arguments? Not at all. He will simply "explicate" the notion of the other, that is, see *what is meant by* "being an alter ego": studying the constitution of the alter ego is to see how this *sense* is fashioned in me.[83] In this way I see that "others" are also objects in the world, natural beings, but that they have in addition for me a particular sense, that of being *"subjects for this world,* as experiencing it." [84] Pursuing intentional analysis, I see that even the other's existence is in some sense more primitive than that of the things of the objective world, because "the existence-sense (*Seinssinn*) [85] of the world and of Nature in particular, as Objective Nature, includes after all . . . thereness-for-everyone." [86] I do not find myself, then, in the presence of natural things, some of which would possess, besides their general character of things, the quite particular character of being the sign of an alien subjectivity. The objective existence of things presupposes, on the contrary, the existence of a plurality of subjects: the object is essentially only an intentional intersubjective unity.[87]

If the object implies the alter ego, the latter in turn implies my own ego (in the sense of a constituted monad, of a psychophysical reality inserted into nature). I will thus have first to specify, in the world as a whole, the zone of what is my own, of my "belongings," and, in contrast, of what is foreign to me. The

82. *Ibid.,* pp. 90 ff.
83. *Ibid.,* p. 90.
84. *Ibid.,* p. 91.
85. Italicized in the original.
86. *CM,* p. 92.
87. "My ego . . . can be a world-experiencing ego only by being in communion with others like himself" (*CM,* p. 139).

other "egos" are then characterized, inside the unique world common to us all, by the different zones to which they belong. The other will be given to me through a kind of mediate intentionality that Husserl calls "appresentation." It indicates a referent, the other's subjectivity, whose proper *sense* is that it "can never become an 'itself-there.' " [88] What is appresented can never really be present: it is the very *sense* of the other that requires my never reaching him in himself: to seek intimate, profound, real unity with the other does not mean aspiring to a state which would be inaccessible to us by virtue of the weakness of our nature; it is *essentially* non-sense. It is both wanting and not wanting the same thing.

Husserl's Fifth Meditation is particularly difficult. The problems it raises are numerous and important. We do not have to consider them at length. It is enough that we have shown that it is by explicating the *sense* of what he was studying that Husserl arrived at the results he offers us. Again, by a series of analogical investigations, he intends to pursue the solution of what still remains problematical. He has never had the pretension of giving a "world system," complete and without gaps. The value of phenomenology comes, on the contrary, from its opening new paths, from its giving us the means to travel them, and from its guiding our way. Transcendental phenomenology intends to preserve this prospective value, which so strongly attracted the early disciples in the years following the publication of the *Logical Investigations*. In assuming the form of a *transcendental idealism* it did not stiffen into dogmatism and lost nothing of its dynamism: on the contrary, it opens to us a field of limitless investigations where it shows us we can progress indefinitely.

The *Cartesian Meditations* must be taken for what they are: the illumination of transcendental subjectivity, the recognition of the life of the ego as constituting the world, and the indication of some of the most urgent work yet to be accomplished. The obscurities found there, which Husserl more than anyone was aware of, could not be dispelled in a few words; this becomes evident from the concrete analyses one must have the courage and the patience to engage in.

88. *Ibid.*, p. 109.

All the problems, however, are not on the same level. There are some which necessarily arise before others. The order of their possible resolution must determine our work plan, rather than the greater or lesser personal interest we may have in regard to this or that question. Phenomenology "by no means professes to stop short of the 'supreme and ultimate questions.'" [89] On the contrary, it will recover all ethical and religious problems, those "of death, of fate, of the possibility of a 'genuine' human life demanded as 'meaningful' in a particular sense—among them, therefore, the problem of the 'meaning' of history—and all the further and still higher problems." [90] Nor does it eliminate existential problems: it only wants to find a sense for them, and this presupposes that certain preliminary analyses have been correctly effected.

We would have liked to give a precise notion of the nature of constitutive investigations and the method of intentional analysis which Husserl applies to it. The latter is indeed characterized: by the search for *sense;* by its method of bringing to light *implications;* by its linking of constituted structures to the *constituting life* of the ego. We do not think it necessary to enumerate the quotations illustrating the first two of these three aspects. [91] The third is by contrast more difficult to elucidate.

We can indeed see in the *Cartesian Meditations* how the structures of the world become progressively intelligible to the extent to which they are connected to the *ego cogito* in a "systematic unitary complex." [92] Phenomenology goes beyond mere eidetic investigation to the extent to which it unifies the elements which were previously scattered and presented to consciousness in a way which was yet somewhat empirical. But "every genuine intuition has its place in the constitutive nexus." [93] Now, if the

89. *Ibid.*, p. 156.
90. *Ibid.*
91. Let us give, however, another typical passage: "In the sense of a *community of men* and in that of *man* . . . there is implicit a *mutual being for one another*" (*CM*, p. 129).
92. *Ibid.*, p. 144.
93. *Ibid.*, p. 138. The method of implication, some essences implying others, and the way in which their system is interrupted at the level of persons, has some similarity to Hamelin's endeavor. For the latter as well, the idea of relation, for example, implies that of number; both "have

noematic side of the intuitions which have their origin in the ego is perfectly clear, their noetic aspect is much less so. What is the final nature of constituting intentionality? Is it experienced as an *Erlebnis* of a superior level, or does it simply form the term of an unfulfilled intention, perhaps even of an intention whose sense forbids its ever being effected? We do know that constitution is something original, but here we are hemmed in by two alternatives: either to say nothing of constitution, since it transcends the world, which is the domain of all language, so that phenomenology ends in a kind of mysticism; or else to speak of it, and so fall back into the world, lowering transcendental idealism to the level of psychological idealism, which, precisely, it claims to oppose. These two possibilities must both be formally rejected. It is between a doctrine of the *world* and a doctrine of *another world* that transcendental phenomenology must find its own path. It continually risks—and this it must remember— falling back into nature or vanishing in the ineffable. It is in no way a comfortable doctrine where one could contentedly settle in; a continual effort is required in order to balance oneself on the narrow ridge which is its proper domain.

Yet we will be able to speak, indeed we must speak, of this constituting life of the ego, but we will be able to do so only analogically,[94] always keeping in mind the essential inadequacy

---

meaning only" through that of time and so forth. But it seems to us that Husserl gives this process its true name in terming it "intentional analysis." There is really nothing properly synthetic, that is, really constructive, in Hamelin's course. Each dialectical moment does not truly create anything new, since the earlier moments have no stability in themselves. Contrary to what Hamelin says about the primacy of synthesis, one would have to say that what he terms thus is possible only by reason of an implicit analysis: the mind was already present when the relation called forth number. We cannot even say that number is "logically" prior to time, precisely since it only has meaning through it. Despite its form, Hamelin's *Essay* is thus only an analytical explication of the *ego cogito* itself; yet it is an intentional explication in the sense that each moment it isolates requires others, calls them forth, and has meaning only through them.

94. We find again here the sole path which seems to be allowed to philosophy, once it is no longer content to merely destroy idols and prejudices—the path Plato opens when he tells us, for example, that, too impure to contemplate the Idea of the Good, we can at least understand that it is to the world of Ideas what the Sun is to the world of bodies or what fire is to the flow of moving shadows. In Plato, myth, like metaphor in Berg-

of all human language in regard to the transcendental.

Granted this, will we have to consider the constituting life of the "I" as analogous to what, in the world, is activity, or, on the contrary, as having at least a formal relation to passivity? On this point Husserl does not provide us with a precise answer.[95]

Certain passages of the *Cartesian Meditations* indicate that two levels will have to be distinguished within transcendental phenomenology itself: a phenomenology of the first degree, still tainted with apodictic naïveté [96]—that is, incapable of fully accounting for the necessity of the structures it elucidates—and an essentially critical phenomenology, charged with "determining not only the *range* and *limits* but also the *modes of apodicticity*." [97] The *Cartesian Meditations* present considerations which proceed sometimes from one, sometimes from the other, of these two disciplines.

But Husserl also alludes to a "static" and a "genetic" explication of intentions [98] and to a difference between "static" and "genetic" constitution.[99] Must genetics be understood here as a world activity, or have we returned to a phenomenology which would be both truly transcendental and yet genetic? Must this genetic phenomenology be considered analogous to the critical phenomenology whose necessity Husserl emphasized at the end

---

son has, among other functions, that of suggesting the unutterable, by using symbols such that we are not in danger of taking them, in their material nature, for the very thing whose feeling they hope to create in us.

95. We have had in our possession the text of a "Sixth Meditation" drafted by Fink, not as the eventual complement to Husserl's five Meditations, but as a document of his own work, intended to serve as a basis for his conversations with Husserl on the point which now holds our attention, that is, in some sense, on "a theory of phenomenological cognition." We obviously could not use here a document such as this one, which presents no definitive ideas and forms a concrete moment of the investigation. In reading it and in having knowledge of certain remarks made by Husserl about it, we see, however, on the one hand, what interest the founder of phenomenology took in these questions, and, on the other, the lack of a precise answer to the question we are asking here. For a phenomenologist, such an answer could not come from an intellectual decision made after a brief examination. It must arise in its time from the patient and progressive development of investigations and concrete analyses.

96. *CM*, p. 151.
97. *Ibid.*, pp. 151–52.
98. *Ibid.*, p. 142.
99. *Ibid.*, p. 135; *Logik*, p. 221.

of the Fifth Meditation? It does not seem possible to answer these ambiguities in any decisive way.

With the documents we have, we can at least understand that we must refrain from too quickly identifying transcendental life with human life. In the strict sense of the terms, and as we have pointed out above,[100] the constituting life of the ego is neither active (for activity, which presupposes time, is in the world), nor passive, for there is absolutely nothing outside the I (since everything is constituted) and in relation to which it could be said to be "passive."

We should reject without reservation superficial interpretations which, in the course of the association of ideas provoked by words belonging to current philosophical language, would risk giving phenomenology a "constructive" aspect, which seems as distant as possible from what it seeks to realize.

Thus *synthesis*, in Husserl, is not a constructive operation. This term simply designates a *systematic unity* which is a "primal form belonging to consciousness." [101] Constituting synthetically (one could even say "syntactically") [102] is understanding that such and such *cogitata* are related to the same intentional object.[103] The syntactical relation is in no way an operation. Here, understanding never means making, or even remaking: unity is "seen" and not constructed; the syntactical connection is grasped by intuition, just as are the essences it connects. In the transcendental sphere, mediations are doubtless established among our cognitions, but these mediations, which are intentional implications, are strictly intuited.[104] Synthesis differs from thesis only as the complex from the simple; and the thesis, the positing, is itself a simple intellectual regard, a simple (*schlichte*) noesis. For Husserl, "positing" has no relation with the practical domain: "rational consciousness in general designates a *summum genus* of thetic modalities." [105]

No more than the word "synthesis" should the term "func-

100. See above, p. 79.
101. *CM*, p. 39.
102. *Ibid.*, p. 42.
103. *Ibid.*, p. 40.
104. Cf. "Nachwort," p. 553.
105. *Ideen*, pp. 285–86.

tion" awaken in us, in connection with phenomenology, the idea of some sort of activity. The central idea it envelops is that of finality. The function of an element is its teleological role in the constitution of a synthetic unity. "Taken in this sense, entirely different from the one it has in mathematics, function . . . is something absolutely original, which has its principle in the *pure essence of the noesis.*" [106]

These remarks on vocabulary confirm what we hoped to grasp of the spirit of the doctrine. They encourage us to persevere in our effort—difficult, but necessary—to preserve constitution in its character of being at once intuitive and creative.

106. *Ibid.,* p. 176.

6 / Husserl, Kant, and Descartes

HISTORICAL STUDIES often conclude with a critical chapter. Here the author reconsiders, in order to demonstrate their inadequacies, the theses he had previously attempted to make intelligible, that is to say, justifiable. We have tried too seriously to follow the movement of Husserlian thought for such a reversal to now seem suitable to us. It seemed preferable to present elsewhere the result of our personal reflections. "De nobis ipsis silemus: de re autem, quae agitur, petimus."

Here we are seeking to make the meaning of transcendental phenomenology more easily grasped. Perhaps we will succeed better in this if we show the similarities and the differences that exist between Husserl's doctrine and those of classical philosophers whom we cannot help thinking of in connection with it. We will limit ourselves here to comparing Husserl to Kant and to Descartes.

Heidegger notes an influence exerted on Husserl by Natorp, the neo-Kantian, in the period between the publication of the *Logische Untersuchungen* and the *Ideen*. During this same time, Husserl claims to have been influenced especially by Descartes. H. de Vleeschauwer[1] and, with some reservations, Edith Stein[2]

1. H.-J. de Vleeschauwer, "La Philosophie contemporaine et le criticisme kantien," paper delivered before the 1st Congrès national des Sociétés françaises de Philosophie, Marseilles, 1938 (*Actes du Congrès*, I, 7).
2. *Journées d'Etudes de la Société Thomiste*, p. 48 (résumé of the discussions devoted to phenomenology held on September 12, 1932).

think that phenomenology owes to Kant the *positio quaestionis.* It seems to us that this is going too far. Kant, for whom Husserl does not, however, hide his esteem, did perhaps help him to realize his own thought and to discover the profound sense of Cartesianism. Kant, Descartes, and Husserl have all three reflected on the *cogito,* but attitude, method, and intention seem to us very similar in the last two and very different in Husserl and in Kant.

What most directly suggests the comparison of phenomenology and critical philosophy is that both employ the same vocabulary: Husserl speaks of the "matter" of cognition and of its "a priori forms"; he presents the subject as "constituting" the world. He has a theory of "synthesis," a doctrine of "categories." But the most important term is certainly "transcendental," one that recurs constantly in his writing. Husserl's logic is a *Formal and Transcendental Logic:* moreover, the most important part of the *Critique of Pure Reason* is also a transcendental logic. The knowing subject is called transcendental in Husserl as in Kant. Finally, both present their doctrine as a "transcendental idealism."

But in each case the same words have quite different meanings. We have already indicated [3] what is signified in Husserl by the term "synthesis," which is absolutely not intended to designate a constructive operation.

In Kant the expression "a priori" designates, not "the cognitions which are independent of such and such an experience, but those which are *absolutely* independent of any experience." [4] The a priori which is thus logically prior to experience, and which constitutes its possibility, consequently becomes inaccessible to experience. There is, on the contrary, in Husserl a particular experience of the a priori, be it material or formal. Husserl retains only a single feature of the Kantian a priori: its necessity; but he will identify it with essence, with the eidos, [5] or with the object,

3. See above, p. 93.
4. *Kritik der reinen Vernunft,* 2d ed., Introduction, p. 3. We refer to the pages of the *Critique* in the original 1st and 2nd editions, this pagination being generally given in most classical editions.
5. Edmund Husserl, *Logik,* p. 219.

taken in its broadest sense, in order to thus include all syntactical objectivities. This is what represents for Husserl "the only one among the multiple meanings of the ambiguous expression a priori" which he intends to adopt, the only one we should bear in mind "whenever it is a question of a priori in my works." [6] What most precisely determines the sense of the Kantian a priori is its opposition to the empirical; yet, this is not retained by phenomenology.

The confusions which could result in connection with the "transcendental" are even more serious. As Fink notes,[7] in Kant this term is in opposition to "empirical," in Husserl, to "world." This is because, in the former, there is a relation between the transcendental and the a priori, while in Husserl the a priori is in the world and is reached through experience. This is not all. In Husserl the transcendental designates a reality. When we speak of the "transcendental subject," contrary to what the expression might suggest, transcendental is not really an adjective, since it can only be applied to the "I."

In Kant, on the contrary, "transcendental" is an epithet which does not even characterize a certain region of being, that of the a priori, for example; it only indicates a certain way of seeing things: "transcendental cognition is not concerned with objects as much as with our *way of knowing* objects, insofar as this should be possible a priori." [8] Transcendental cognition is thus not in any way a direct apprehension but a critical reflection. It is not the revelation of an absolute reality, even that of an act; it means bringing to light a priori conditions without which no cognition could be possible. But this philosophical elaboration is made in the world. By it man acquires no new faculty and has no access to the unknowable transcendence of things in themselves. Those who would like to know them would

6. *Ibid.*

7. E. Fink, "Die phänom., p. 376.

8. *Kritik der reinen Vernunft*, 2d ed., Introduction, p. 25. The first edition said that "transcendental cognition is not concerned with objects as much as with our a priori concepts of objects in general." This does not change the character of formal reflection which we want to emphasize: transcendental cognition is not the immediate apprehension of synthetic acts; it is a reflection on the a priori.

have to satisfy their curiosity by means "of a magical art" of which Kant understands nothing.[9]

The subordinate order of the transcendental and the transcendent is reversed in phenomenology: the transcendent is in the world: it is simply what surpasses the actual content of psychological consciousness.[10] But transcendence and immanence have meaning only for and through the transcendental, which is beyond the world and which constitutes all world meanings, including the meaning of the transcendent.

Hence, an identical vocabulary conceals profoundly different philosophical attitudes. Kant and Husserl contrast initially in their starting points. As Edith Stein notes, "neo-Kantianism starts with the *fact of sciences* and from them transcendentally deduces their conditions."[11] In so doing, it only accentuates Kant's position: it is because "mathematical judgments are all synthetic"[12] and because "physics contains a priori synthetic judgments as principles"[13] that he is led to ask his essential question: "How are a priori synthetic judgments possible?"[14] And it is not the *idea* of science that has hold of him, this ideal of certainty and intelligibility that preoccupies Husserl in his *Logic;* it is science as it actually is: Euclidean geometry and Newtonian physics. Charles Serrus has well shown [15] the fragility this basis gives to the theses of transcendental aesthetics. But the transcendental analytic does not emerge unscathed from the confrontation of the aesthetic with contemporary science: the unifying synthesis is necessary solely because sense experience gives us only, according to Bréhier's expression, "scattered diversity."[16] The representation of the mind that Kant makes for himself comes from the idea he has of physics:

9. *Kritik der reinen Vernunft,* 1st ed., Preface, p. VII.
10. See above, pp. 35, 36.
11. *Journées d'Etudes de la Société Thomiste,* p. 46.
12. *Kritik der reinen Vernunft,* 2d ed., Introduction, p. 14.
13. *Ibid.,* p. 17.
14. *Ibid.,* p. 19.
15. Charles Serrus, *L'Esthétique transcendentale et la science moderne* (Paris: Alcan, 1930).
16. Emile Bréhier, *Histoire de la philosophie* (Paris: Alcan, 1930), II, 530.

It does not seem questionable that Kant took as a model of cognition that aspect of cognition which had been made familiar by Newtonian physics: on the one hand, a series of scattered events, acquired independently of one another; on the other hand, a concept or a law which the mind discovers and which creates the connection or the union of these events; on the one hand, then, passively accumulated material, and on the other, an active intelligence which ties these events together in order to think them.[17]

If he retains science as an ideal, Husserl, in contrast, rejects sciences as data. They are only attempts at interpretation beyond which one must return to the "things themselves." It is thus necessary to "go back to prescientific data," [18] to return to naïvely experiencing the world,[19] whose structure we will have, not to deduce, but to reveal. It is starting from this personal and concrete experience that scientific theories will be able to work out their proper meanings: it is starting from the original sense my body has for me that the general sense of any animal body whatever will be able to be clarified.[20]

Opposed in their points of departure, Kant and Husserl are no less opposed in the idea each makes for himself of the mind and its powers. The distinction of the passive affection of sense and the synthetic activity of the mind, fundamental in Kant, is not found in Husserl, for whom understanding is intuitive and for whom the ego does not allow itself to be subdivided into particular faculties. Husserl's confidence in reason is absolute: the thing-in-itself is absurd. Kant deems it necessary and thus preserves the rights of a "beyond the knowable" in connection with which we will, however, be able to accept what will be demanded by practical reason, on the single condition that these *beliefs,*

17. *Ibid.,* pp. 519–20.
18. E. Stein, in *Journées d'Etudes de la Société Thomiste,* p. 46.
19. L. Landgrebe and J. Patocka, "Edmund Husserl zum Gedächtnis," *Schriften des Prager Philosophischen Cercles* (Prague: Academia Verlagsbuchhandlung, 1938), p. 27.
20. "The earth could no more lose its sense as 'the primal place where one is at home,' as the principle (ἀρχή) of the world, than my body could lose its absolutely unique sense as primal body, from which every body (*Leib*) draws a part of its existential sense" (Edmund Husserl, manuscript, p. 21, transcribed by Landgrebe, classified in the Husserl Archives as D, 17, under the title *Die Ur-Arche Erde bewegt sich nicht*).

thus substituted for *knowledge*,[21] be accepted as possible by theoretical thought. We have seen that, in contrast to this primacy of practical reason, Husserl opposes a clear primacy of theoretical reason.[22]

As for their manner of proceeding, Kant and Husserl could not be more dissimilar. The latter sees and describes what the former constructs. The suppleness—perhaps excessive—of Husserl, careful to free himself from prejudices, seeing in language simply a means of suggestion, of calling upon personal experience, and denouncing without hesitation all that is artificial and distorted in the efforts of other scholars to establish a definitive vocabulary, is in contrast to the rigidity of Kant, who hopes that his system will preserve after him its "invariable fixity." [23] If we refuse to confuse evidence with the guarantee of certainty, as Husserl himself refused to do in his last works, we see that an intuitive apprehension of categories preserves the possibilities of a science to come, an attitude impossible for a theory apprehending these same categories as immutable laws of thought.

If we limit ourselves to the particular problem which forms the object of our study, we will find differences just as profound between Husserl's transcendental subject and the Kantian subject. The first is a concrete, indubitable reality, grasped in its originary power by an immediate intuition. It is the *real* origin from which everything proceeds. For Kant we cannot even "say of the I that it is a concept; it is a simple consciousness (*blosses Bewusstsein*) which accompanies all concepts." [24] The "I" is no longer anything real; it is only the a priori condition of knowledge. To think is to judge,[25] that is, to join by a synthetic act. Different manners of thinking will thus necessarily correspond to different manners of judging, that is, of joining. It is indeed evident, then, that they all suppose joining in general. In this way, we go from sciences to categories, from categories to the

21. *Kritik der reinen Vernunft*, 2d ed., Preface, p. XXX.
22. See above, pp. 79 ff.
23. *Kritik der reinen Vernunft*, 2d ed., Preface, p. XXXVIII.
24. *Ibid.*, p. 404.
25. The power to judge is "the same thing as the power to think" (*Kritik der reinen Vernunft*, 2d ed., p. 106). "Thinking is the same thing as judging" (Prolegomena, § 22).

"I think" which is their "vehicle," [26] and, accessorily, from the "I think" to the subject, to the "I," whose spontaneity is manifested in the joinings. Kant will be concerned with this "I" particularly in order to dispute its ontological interpretation: the permanent subject of thought is only a logical subject [27] which we tend to take for a real subject.[28] We could not have an intuition of it; [29] every intuition in effect refers to sense experience.[30] Thus, we cannot know it, since knowing—which is other than thinking— always refers definitively to possible intuitions.[31]

Hence the subject is not experienced; it is conceded. It is only a formal condition. The *Opus Postumum* itself, which undeniably has idealist tendencies (whether they convey a profound intention of the system, or whether they manifest a displacement of perspective under the influence of critics), preserves the logical character of the "I." [32] The "I think," a universal form, has lost the aspect of a static given that it had in the *Critique* only to take on that "of an act and of a becoming"; [33] but it is still a logical act.[34]

Yet if the subject were not logical from a Kantian point of view, one does not see what it could be. Kant recognizes nothing

26. *Kritik der reinen Vernunft*, 2d ed., pp. 399, 406.
27. "Thus it is certain that, by the I, I always represent to myself an absolute but logical unity of the subject (simplicity) but that I do not in any way know, as a result, the real simplicity of my subject" (*Kritik der reinen Vernunft*, 1st ed., p. 356). "*I am simple* does not signify any more than the fact, for this representation, *I*, of not concealing the least diversity and being an absolute unity (although purely logical)" (*ibid.*, p. 355).
28. *Ibid.*, p. 350.
29. "The I is indeed in all thoughts; but there is not connected to this representation the least intuition which would distinguish the I from other objects of intuition" (*ibid.*, p. 350).
30. "Our nature requires that intuition be never other than sensible" (*Kritik der reinen Vernunft*, 2d ed., p. 75).
31. *Ibid.*, p. 747.
32. See, in particular, *Opus Postumum*, in the new, complete edition of A. Buchenau (Berlin and Leipzig, 1936 and 1938), II, 79 (apperception is presented here as "a purely logical act"); pp. 83, 85, 89, 90, 91 ("I am the thinking subject but I am not the object of intuition because I cannot yet know myself"); pp. 93, 95 ("the logical act *I think*, or apperception . . ."); pp. 98, 100, 102. Cf. H.-J. de Vleeschauwer, *La Déduction transcendentale dans l'oeuvre de Kant*, III, 620 ff.
33. *Ibid.*, p. 617.
34. *Ibid.*, p. 618.

between the noumenon and the phenomenon. The critique of the paralogisms of pure reason warns us against likening the "I" to a substance; but, on the other hand, making the "I" a phenomenon would be confusing transcendental knowledge with psychological knowledge. The "I," then, can only be formal; it will be "the simple form of consciousness" [35] and, doubtless, the most elevated form, which all others presuppose.

What Kant does not clarify and what Husserl thinks he has exhibited is a particular mode of existence proper to the subject: for Husserl, the "I" is real without being substantial. The transcendental is no longer a certain manner of knowing, characterizing our reflection on the a priori elements of the world; it is rather an original manner of being, of *being outside the world*. Contrary to what the word "phenomenon" could lead us to believe, appearing in the name it applies to itself, phenomenology, like traditional metaphysics, has a constant preoccupation, the nostalgia of being.[36] But by its theory of intentionality it avoids the incomprehensible relation of the substance "self" and external substances, "absurd things-in-themselves": primal consciousness, due to its intentional nature, offers us access to absolutely true being.[37]

Is it legitimate, however, to see in Kantianism a simple formalism? Kant once became angry upon hearing Schlosser call criticism a manufacturing of forms.[38] Form is not an act but a product. It must thus be carried back to its principle, that is, to the subject, understood as a real, constructive activity. De Vleeschauwer believes that Kant did, indeed, attain this point of view but that he did not remain at this level and "continually fell back into the symbolism of abstract logic." [39] "Because it has seen this only at intervals and has forgotten it at least as often, the deduction combines nonassimilable tendencies, and all sorts of problems are grafted onto this original flaw of Kantian deduction." [40]

35. *Kritik der reinen Vernunft*, 1st ed., p. 382.
36. Cf. E. Fink, "Das Problem der Phänomenologie Edmund Husserls," *Revue internationale de Philosophie*, I, No. 2 (1939), 226–70.
37. *Ibid.*, p. 248.
38. H.-J. de Vleeschauwer, *La Déduction transcendentale dans l'oeuvre de Kant*, III, 287.
39. *Ibid.*, p. 288.
40. *Ibid.*

Without ignoring these contraditions, Lachièze-Rey believes it is possible, in the light of the *Opus Postumum*, to recognize in all of Kant's work, even as early as the *Critique of Pure Reason*, "an essential theory necessarily called upon to subordinate and order all others, the theory of the construction of the self and the world under the aegis of the constructing mind." [41] We do not have to examine in itself this interpretation, which permits Kantianism to transcend formalism. Let us ask only whether it authorizes us to see in phenomenology a return to criticism. Can we find in the Husserlian *cogito* the equivalent of this immediate consciousness of synthetic activity?

In connection with phenomenology, we can undoubtedly employ once more Brunschvicg's apt formula and say that "knowing oneself is grasping oneself in one's constituting power." [42] But in Husserl this is not a constructive power. We willingly recognize that it is difficult to explicate the phenomenological theory of constitution in a way which does not leave it open to criticism. Most of the texts that refer to it are unpublished and are personal notes in which the vocabulary is still less unified than in the published works. We believe that constitution must be interpreted on the basis of all we know of Husserl's general attitude and upon what is specified in the *Ideen* or the *Cartesian Meditations*. For Husserl, constituting is not "making"; [43] and in the grasp of being which is evidence we are neither dominant nor dominated.

Doubtless for Lachièze-Rey the act of the self is not necessarily limited to constructing. [44] But this means, as he clearly indicates, broadening the Kantian conception. There, the act is essentially constructive: being, for the subject, is making. One could even say that what critical philosophy essentially proposes resides in this construction more than in the recognition of the self by itself. The method at work, then, is "a *reflexive analysis;* it is from science, taken as fact, that it departs in order to rise to the a priori forms of intuition, to the pure concepts of the under-

41. P. Lachièze-Rey, *L'Idéalisme kantien* (Paris: Alcan, 1931), p. 2.
42. L. Brunschvicg, *L'Expérience humaine et la causalité physique* (Paris: Alcan, 1922), p. 612.
43. See above, pp. 77 ff.
44. P. Lachièze-Rey, *L'Idéalisme kantien*, p. 58.

standing." [45] But beyond the discovery of an a priori which only transposes to the absolute the contingent forms of Newtonian science, the critical idea that is most fertile is

> the discovery of a capacity of intellectual invention, of scientific creation, which, because it rises from consciousness in accordance with the human order, and not from reason in accordance with the divine order, never manifests its true character better than by breaking the mold of forms and the letter of laws in which we had first thought it to be . . . imprisoned.[46]

Thus, whatever theory is emphasized in an interpretation of Kantianism, the difference from phenomenology remains no less profound. Husserl is opposed to formalism as much as he is to construction. He does not start from the sciences but places them in brackets, just as he does common-sense assertions. Far from substituting the human order of scientific judgment for the divine order of atemporal essences, he places his transcendental ego beyond the human.[47]

Must we conclude from this that Kant had no notion of the originary power of the transcendental subject which had so keenly struck Husserl? Certainly not; and for evidence we need only refer to the difficulty involved in forming an idea of the nature of the "I" from Kant's texts. Perhaps no other point of critical philosophy allows more diverse interpretations. This is because Kant's central interest was not directed to this point; and this, moreover, is what distinguishes him most from Husserl. Preoccupied by the sciences and by the foundation of objectivity, Kant elicits the conditions that both presuppose. But he does not particularly ask himself in what way these conditions are known. What is to be understood by "simple consciousness"? What is a representation that is neither a concept nor an intuition? What is a "simple apprehension"? [48] How can the "I" be an intellectual

45. L. Brunschvicg, "L'Idée critique et le système kantien," *Revue de métaphysique et de morale*, XXXI, No. 2 (1924), 153.
46. *Ibid.*, p. 159.
47. In examining the conditions of knowledge, Kant often places himself in an anthropological perspective: it is possible that all finite beings are submitted to the same conditions as we; but we are not in a position to decide this. Kant's theory of knowledge is valid for men.
48. *Opus Postumum*, II, 89.

representation without, however, being a concept? [49] Kant seems to have felt that knowledge of the "I" could not be formed according to the modes he had himself imposed upon all knowledge. Husserl is thus completely warranted in saying that "Kant is on the road" to true transcendental philosophy as he himself understands it.[50]

A final trait will serve to point out the difference that exists between Kant's position and that of Husserl: it is the reciprocal manner in which the neo-Kantians and the phenomenologists accuse each other of dogmatism. For the former group,[51] phenomenology remains dogmatic because it wants to be a philosophy of intuition (whereas every intuition presupposes a subjacent construction) and also because it remains caught in the snares of an illusory metaphysics and gives an ontological value to the "I" instead of seeing there a pure form, a nonontological subject.[52] Husserl's conversion to Kantianism loses its interest if it is not complete: ontology is the antithesis of critical philosophy.[53]

Phenomenology, on the contrary, claims to be the sole philosophy that truly escapes dogmatism. It is just as dogmatic to prefer construction to intuition as to do the reverse. The essential thing is not to do it spontaneously, without preliminary reflection. Dogmatism is natural "naïveté," that of the scientist as well as that of the man in the street. They are both involved "in the world" and accept, without calling into question, all that habit and tradition have slowly deposited in their minds, without their being aware of it.[54] Doubt alone frees from dogmatism, yet

49. "The consciousness of self in the representation *I* is not at all an intuition but a simple intellectual representation of the spontaneity of a thinking subject" (*Kritik der reinen Vernunft*, 2d ed., p. 278).

50. Edmund Husserl, "Krisis," p. 174; *Krisis*, p. 102; *Crisis*, p. 99.

51. See, for example, R. Zocher, *Husserls Phänomenologie und Schuppes Logik* (Munich, 1932), *passim.* Cf. E. Fink, "Die phänom.," pp. 325 ff.

52. Zocher, *Husserls Phänom.*, p. 20; E. Fink, "Die phänom.," p. 335. H. Richert, who inspired Zocher, also clearly characterizes the transcendental as unreal and purely formal (*Der Gegenstand der Erkenntnis* [Tübingen, 1928], p. 50). Hence, he chooses to see in phenomenology only a "transcendental psychology" (*ibid.*, p. 300).

53. Zocher, *Husserls Phänomenologie und Schuppes Logik*, p. 14.

54. Let us look, for example, at the pages in which Husserl seeks to

Kant did not surrender himself to doubt in a sufficiently radical manner. In a certain sense one can say that Hume doubted for him. But doubt is neither the simple introduction to problems to be resolved nor the opportunity for dialectical exercises. It is an ordeal we must undergo personally: one cannot make use of another's doubt. This original experience has a purificatory value: "anyone who seriously intends to become a philosopher must 'once in his life' withdraw into himself and attempt, within himself, to overthrow and build anew all the sciences that, up to then, he has been accepting. Philosophy—wisdom [sagesse]—is the philosopher's quite personal affair." [55]

If doubt is the essential moment of phenomenology, it is not in Kantianism, where "the idea of constitution is still worldly," [56] that Husserl will seek inspiration. In certain respects, Hume's reflection is more penetrating than Kant's; yet "Hume, as understood by Kant, is not the true Hume." [57] But, beyond Hume, it is to Descartes that we must return: "Kant never allowed himself to descend into the immense depths of fundamental Cartesian reflection, nor did his own problems lead him to seek ultimate decisions and justifications in these depths." [58]

We have already had the opportunity, in the course of this work, to show all that is similar in the attitudes of Husserl and Descartes. We would like to restrict ourselves now to comparing, in the two philosophers, the nature of the doubt which precedes the *cogito* and the nature of the subject asserting itself in the *cogito*.

What corresponds in Husserl to the Cartesian doubt is phenomenological reduction; both of these courses are lived experiences, personal adventures. Overly occupied with an examination of the Cartesian "system," carried along by the "prospective" movement of Cartesianism, we are too much inclined to neglect

---

show the traditional character of geometry: E. Husserl, "Die Frage nach dem Ursprung der Geometrie als intentional-historisches Problem," *Revue internationale de philosophie*, I, No. 2 (1939), 207–25.

55. Edmund Husserl, *CM*, p. 2.
56. E. Fink, "Die phänom.," p. 375.
57. "Krisis," p. 171; *Krisis*, p. 99; *Crisis*, p. 95. See our study on "Husserl et Hume," *Revue internationale de philosophie*, I, No. 2 (1939), 342–53.
58. "Krisis," p. 174; *Krisis*, p. 102; *Crisis*, p. 99.

everything that precedes the *cogito*, or, at least, we see in it only the indication of difficulties to be overcome; whereas each one of us must perform for himself a total reversal, an overthrow. Phenomenological reduction methodically retraces the stages of this liberation through doubt.

But is it possible to call everything into question? Husserl and Descartes seem to retain an absolute confidence in the power of reason and exclude it from reduction.[59] They do not justify their rationalism. But what value could an examination have which does not consider the very thing one wanted to examine? Here one cannot demonstrate; one can only make visible, unveil. It is in this sense that Descartes attempts to establish the existence of God, guarantor of the rationality of the universe.[60] In an analogous manner, Husserl's rationalism is made explicit in the analyses by which he seeks to have the primacy of theoretical thought acknowledged,[61] to show that it is implied by all possible modes of thought.

Yet this confidence is not maintained *despite* doubt. It is found again *after* doubt. We regain confidence when we again lay hold of the *cogito;* but we have known anguish. Phenomenology has its own drama: [62] it unfolds in doubt, when we have lost the *natural* sense of the world, before having found its *transcendental* sense.[63] Phenomenological anguish is not a superficial aspect of existential anguish, as would be that of a man worried about the limits of his intelligence. It is deeper than existential anguish, which is that of an individual in the world.

59. "The confidence Husserl has in reason is limitless" (Illeman, *Husserls vorphänomenologische Philosophie* [Leipzig, 1932], p. 41). Cf. also Chestov, "Qu'est-ce que la vérité?," *Revue philosophique*, II, No. 1 (1927), 36–74.

60. The atheist does not know by way of a true and certain science that the sum of the angles of a triangle is equal to two right angles (*Réponses aux deuxièmes objections*, Adam and Tannery, VII, 141. Cf. *Réponses aux troisièmes objections*, Adam and Tannery, VII, 428, and IX, 230).

61. See, above, pp. 79 ff.

62. It is clearly presented by E. Fink, "Was will . . . ," pp. 18 ff. "It is madness to confuse the fundamental rational passion of philosophy with the tranquil attitude of someone who surrenders himself to an intellectual game" (*ibid.*, p. 20).

63. Husserl has personally and painfully lived this drama and was about to abandon teaching a discipline whose sense escaped him.

Phenomenological reduction does not appear in all this as an original step: it only takes up again—a little more rigorously, a little more ponderously as well—Descartes's endeavor. It distinguishes itself from the latter, however, on a point which to us does not seem the essential one. In order to better insure himself against error, Descartes wants to reject as absolutely false everything in which he can imagine the slightest doubt.[64] His attempt at universal doubt is thus an attempt at universal negation.[65] Husserl wants to limit himself to a simple "suspension" of judgment. We cannot really, whatever our desire, seriously believe that the world does not exist. But we can abstract from this existence and reserve our judgment in respect to it. By operating in this way, we are neither sophists nor skeptics.[66] We abstain only from using the evidences the world continues to offer us.[67] The way Husserl presents things in the Cartesian Meditations lessens what separates him from Descartes. It is, indeed, to doubt that the phenomenologist surrenders himself when he seeks apodictic evidence, that is, "absolute indubitability." [68] A difference remains, however: the evidence of the world is never abandoned; it is only subordinated to its principle, after having been held in suspension.

Somewhat different in their way of handling doubt, Husserl and Descartes are reunited in the manner in which they assure the cogito: the "I think" is not a fact one experiences,[69] it is not an

64. Discours de la Méthode, Part 4, Adam and Tannery, VI, 31; Méditations II, Adam and Tannery, IX, 18 and 19, and VI, 24.
65. Edmund Husserl, Ideen, 3d ed., p. 55.
66. Ibid., p. 56.
67. Ibid., p. 57.
68. CM, p. 15.
69. French philosophy has a natural tendency to interpret the cogito as a "datum of consciousness." At the least, it hopes to see there both "a datum of consciousness and a truth of reason" (Lachelier, "Lettre à Ravaisson," December 5, 1859, Correspondance, p. 41). We see here the influence of a tradition that is very French, that of the moralists, turned toward the study of the soul through internal observation. Admittedly, Descartes identified the "I" and the soul, but it is after the cogito that he falls back into this confusion. Maine de Biran, whose philosophy both expresses and reinforces this French "psychologism," was well aware of all that separates him from a Descartes, "always seeking this rational evidence which alone he wants to acknowledge, because he has substituted it for de facto and sensible evidence in the first phenomenon of

existence one grasps, it is the *truth* of an existence recognized by an intuition of the intelligence.[70]

It is here that Husserl and Descartes decidedly part company and that phenomenology widens the horizon of Cartesianism. Descartes does not recognize several different types of existence.[71] When he says "I am," "God is," "the world is," he does not distinguish in each case the original meaning of the word "to be." For him, to be is always "to be a substance." Knowledge will thus henceforth be a modification of the attributes of thinking substance: the soul grasps immediately only its own states, whence the artificial problem of the existence of an *external* world, which divine veracity will have to guarantee.

Husserl reproaches Descartes for not having effected "reduction" rigorously enough and for having preserved for the "I" qualities belonging only to the soul, that is, to psychophysiological man. The criticism seems too severe to us. Descartes's "I" is not man,[72] and the French philosopher seems to us to have reached the purity of the transcendental. But he immediately debases it because he has not seen the intentional character of knowledge.

The crucial problem of idealism, that of knowing how one can go outside individual consciousness, does not exist for phenomenology. We are never "locked" inside consciousness, as if cut off from a mysterious transcendence, because the nature of consciousness is to be directed toward something other than itself. The first truth is not "I think, therefore I am," but *"ego–cogito–cogitatum."* As for the individual, we have left him in the world, body and soul. The recognition of the intentional character of consciousness frees us from the old belief, which was at the basis of sympathetic magic, according to which only like can

---

consciousness" ("Essai sur les fondements de la psychologie," in *Oeuvres inédites,* ed. Naville [Paris, 1859], I, 157–58). Schopenhauer will also note that the French call the transcendental method the psychological method, and this in a rather imprecise way (*Parerga et Paralipomena,* II, Chap. I, § 10; in the Reclam edition [Leipzig, 1895], this will be found in Volume II, page 16).

70. "The soul knows itself only through the pure understanding" ("Lettre à Elisabeth," June 28, 1643, ed. Adam and Tannery, III, 692).

71. At least he does not do so in full consciousness.

72. Let us remember in particular how man is "reduced" in the *Recherche de la vérité.*

know like. Descartes anticipated intentionality; [73] he nevertheless upheld the theory of ideas as copies.[74] Hence the great movement he initiated in order to escape dogmatism [75] missed its mark. He advises us to avoid haste, yet he is impatient to construct a valid science. His desire to make man "the master and possessor of nature" [76] subordinates—in fact, if not in theory—contemplation to technique and removes metaphysics to the mere antechamber of physics. The rationality of the universe must no longer serve to separate us from the sensible and to make us anticipate the perfection of being but must allow us to act in the world with increased effectiveness. Descartes is turned toward the world. There is nothing astonishing in his believing he had saved, by the *cogito*, a small part of the world, from which one will be able to infer, by reasoning, the reality of the rest.

But the transcendental ego is outside the world. To be sure, it is turned toward the world, but in an original manner and without being a part of it, since it has "reduced" individuality. All its *egological* [77] life is composed only of intentionality and of its numerous aspects. These form the "infinite field of transcendental experience," [78] which phenomenology wants to traverse and to describe. One cannot say that Descartes was ignorant of this domain if one believes the words he puts in the mouth of Poliandre in the final lines of what has reached us of the *Search for Truth:* "There are so many things contained in the idea of a thinking thing that entire days would be needed to explicate them." [79]

73. For example, to the extent to which the union of soul and body seems to form a third order, more real in certain respects than that of thought or that of extension. Sometimes extension also receives its sense, in his eyes, from its relation to the subject. Intuition, finally, is a regard and not something immediate.

74. "Natural light made me know with evidence that ideas are in me like paintings or images" (*Third Meditation,* ed. Adam and Tannery, IX, 33).

75. Jean Lacroix very aptly emphasizes that "Cartesian doubt has as its aim freeing us from all dogmatism" ("La signification du doute cartésien," *Rivista di filosofia neo-scolastica,* July, 1937, p. 549).

76. *Discours de la Méthode,* Part 6, ed. Adam and Tannery, VI, 62.

77. "Krisis," p. 157; *Krisis,* p. 84; *Crisis,* p. 82.

78. *CM,* p. 31.

79. *Recherche de la vérité,* ed. Adam and Tannery, X, 527 (trans. Bridoux, *Oeuvres de Descartes* [Paris: Bibliothèque de la Pléiade, 1937], p. 690).

Bibliography

I. WORKS OF EDMUND HUSSERL

"Über den Begriff der Zahl." *Habilitations-schrift.* Halle: F. Beyer, 1887. 64 pp.

Arithmetik   *Philosophie der Arithmetik,* Part 1 (only part published): *Psychologische und logische Untersuchungen.* 1st ed. Halle: Pfeffer, 1891). XVI + 324 pp. 2d ed., published without changes, Leipzig: Kröner.

"Folgerungskalkül und Inhaltslogik." *Vierteljahrsschrift für wissenschaftliche Philosophie,* XV (1891), 168–89 and 351–56.

"A. Voigts Elementare Logik und meine Darlegungen zur Logik der logischen Calculs." *Vierteljahrsschrift für wissenschaftliche Philosophie,* XVII (1893), 11–120 and 508–11.

"Psych. Studien"   "Psychologische Studien zur elementaren Logik." *Philosophische Monatshefte,* XXX (1894), 159–91.

"Bericht über deutsche Schriften zur Logik aus dem Jahre 1894." *Archiv für systematische Philosophie,* III (1897), 216–44.

"Bericht über deutsche Schriften zur Logik

aus dem Jahren 1895–1898." *Archiv für systematische Philosophie*, IX (1903), 113–32, 237–59, 393–408, 523–43. "Bericht über deutsche Schriften zur Logik aus dem Jahren 1895–1899." *Archiv für systematische Philosophie*, X (1904), 101–25.

Log. Unt.   *Logische Untersuchungen*, 1st ed. Halle: Niemeyer, Vol. I (1900), Vol. II (1901). 3rd and 4th eds., 1922 and 1928, without changes.

"Selbstanz."   "Selbstanzeige der Logischen Untersuchungen." *Vierteljahrsschrift für wissenschaftliche Philosophie*, XXIV (1900), 511; XXV (1901), 260–63.

"Phil. als str. Wiss."   "Philosophie als strenge Wissenschaft." *Logos*, I (1911), 289–341.

Ideen   *Ideen zu einer reinen Phänomenologie und phänomenologischen Philosophie* (1st part alone was published). *Jahrbuch für Philosophie und phänomenologische Forschung*, I (1913). 2d and 3d editions published separately without changes.

The English translation of the *Ideen* (New York, 1931) was preceded by an original preface of Edmund Husserl, later published in German, without serious revisions, under the title "Nachwort zu meinen *Ideen* . . ." (see below).

"Erinnerungen an Franz Brentano," pp. 153–67 in *Oskar Kraus, Franz Brentano*. Munich, 1919.

"A. Reinach: Ein Nachruf." *Kantstudien*, XXIII (1919), 147–49.

"Erneuerung: Ihr Problem und ihre Methode." Japanese periodical *Kaizo* (1922), 84–92.

"Idee einer philosophischen Kultur." *Japanisch-deutsche Zeitschrift für Wissenschaft und Technik*, I (1923), 45–51.

"Phenomenology." Article in the *Encyclo-*

paedia Britannica, 14th ed. (1927), XVII, 699–702.

"Vorlesungen zur Phänomenologie des inneren Zeitbewusstseins," edited by Martin Heidegger. *Jahrbuch für Philosophie und phänomenologische Forschung*, IX (1928), 367–496. Published again separately, Halle: Niemeyer, 1929.

Logik   "Formale und transzendentale Logik." *Jahrbuch für Philosophie und phänomenologische Forschung*, X (1929), XI + 298 pp. Published separately, Halle: Niemeyer, 1929.

"Nachwort"   "Nachwort zu meinen *Ideen zu einer reinen Phänomenologie und phänomenologischen Philosophie.*" *Jahrbuch für Philosophie und phänomenologische Forschung*, XI (1930), 549–70. Published separately, Halle: Niemeyer, 1930.

CM   *Cartesian Meditations: An Introduction to Phenomenology*, translated into English by Dorion Cairns (The Hague, 1960).

"Brief an den VIII internationalen Kongress für Philosophie in Prague," pp. XLI–XLV in VIIIe *Congrès international de Philosophie*. Prague, 1936.

"Krisis,"   "Die Krisis der europäischen Wissen-
Krisis,   schaften und die transzendentale Phä-
and   nomenologie, Part 1 (only part pub-
Crisis [1]   lished). *Philosophia*, I (Belgrade, 1936), 77–176.

Erfahrung und Urteil: Untersuchungen zur Genealogie der Logik. Texts written by Husserl, completed and joined together by L. Landgrebe, in accordance with the indications of Husserl himself. Prague: Akademia-Verlag, 1939. XXIV + 478 pp.

"Die Frage nach dem Ursprung der Geome-

1. [For an explanation of these abbreviations, see Chapter 1, footnote 4.—Translator.]

trie als intentional-historisches Problem."
Revue internationale de philosophie, I,
No. 2 (1939), 207–25.

We feel it is useful to add to this list a very important text of
Eugen Fink, written by him under the direct inspiration of Husserl and which appeared in *Kantstudien* preceded by Husserl's
Preface, indicating that the article had been written according
to his wishes and that it contained nothing he did not recognize
as precisely expressing his own thought:

E. Fink, "Die   Eugen Fink. "Die phänomenologische Phi-
phänom."   losophie Edmund Husserls in der gegen-
                    wärtigen Kritik." *Kantstudien,* XXXVIII,
                    No. 3–4 (1933), 319–83.

II. Books And Articles Referring to Edmund Husserl

An extensive bibliography of the books devoted to Edmund
Husserl and to his phenomenology has been published by Jan
Patocka in the *Revue internationale de philosophie,* I, No. 2
(January 15, 1939). We refer the reader to this list and content
ourselves here with indicating a few works which escaped Pa-
tocka's collation or which appeared after its publication.

Abbreviations used:

RPh   *Revue philosophique*
RMM   *Revue de métaphysique et de morale*
EP   *Les Etudes philosophiques*
RIP   *Revue internationale de philosophie*
JP   *The Journal of Philosophy*
NRF   *Nouvelle revue française*

Anonymous obituary notice. "Edmund Husserl." *Riv. di filosofia*
(Milan), XXVII (1938), 365–69.
Anonymous obituary notice. "Husserl." *RMM,* XLV, No. 3 (July,
1938), supplement, pp. 33–34.
A. Banfi. "La Fenomenologia e il compito del pensiero contem-
poraneo." *RIP,* I, No. 2 (January 15, 1939), 326–41.
Cayetano Betancur. "Edmundo Husserl." *Boletín de la Universi-
dad católica bolivariana,* No. 2 (1938), 418–19.
Gaston Berger. "Husserl et Hume." *RIP,* I, No. 2 (January 15,
1939), 242–53.

————. "Quelques aspects de la philosophie allemande contemporaine." *EP*, X, No. 3–4 (December, 1936), 68–74.

Emile Bréhier. *Histoire de la philosophie allemande.* 2d rev. ed. Paris: Vrin, 1933. 186 pp.

Dorion Cairns. "Some Results of Husserl's Investigations." *JP*, XXXVI, No. 9 (April 27, 1939), 236–38.

Antonio Caso. "Edmundo Husserl y la filosofía inglés." *Luminar* (Mexico), II (1938), 177–83.

Léon Chestov. "Qu'est-ce que la vérité?" *RPh*, CIII (January–February, 1927), 36–74.

————. "Memento Mori: A propos de la théorie de la connaissance de Husserl." *RPh*, CI (January–February, 1926), 5–62.

Max Dessoir. "La Phénoménologie de Husserl." *RIP*, I, No. 2 (January 15, 1939), 271–76.

Yanne Feldman-Comiti. "Structures intellectuelles: Introduction à l'étude phénoménologique de l'image. A propos d'un ouvrage récent." *RMM*, XLIV, No. 4 (October, 1937), 767–79.

Eugen Fink. "Das Problem der Phänomenologie Edmund Husserls." *RIP*, I, No. 2 (January 15, 1939), 226–70.

Benjamin Fondane. *La Conscience malheureuse.* Paris: Denoël & Steele, 1936. 307 pp.

Horace L. Friess. "Husserl's Unpublished Manuscripts." *JP*, XXXVI, No. 9 (1939), 238–39.

Rubin Gotesky. "Husserl's Conception of Logic as Kunstlehre in the *Logische Untersuchungen.*" *The Philosophical Review* (New York), XLVII (July, 1938), 375–89.

Aron Gurwitsch. *Phänomenologie der Thematik und des reinen Ich: Studien über Beziehungen von Gestalttheorie und Phänomenologie.* Dissertation presented at Göttingen on August 1, 1928, and published in *Psychologische Forschung*, XII, No. 4 (1929), 279–381.

Kenneth G. Hamilton. "Edmund Husserl's Contribution to Philosophy." *JP*, XXXVI, No. 9 (1939), 225–32.

Charles Hartshorne. "The Method of Imaginative Variations." *JP*, XXXVI, No. 9 (1939), 233–34.

Hans Hegg. *Das Verhältnis der phänomenologischen Lehre von Edmund Husserl zur empirischen Psychologie.* Dissertation defended at Berne on December 1, 1919. Heidelberg: L. Hahn, 1920. 59 pp.

Jean Hering. "Phénoménologie et philosophie religieuse." *Revue d'histoire et de philosophie religieuse* (Strasbourg and Paris), VI, No. 1 (January–February, 1926), 73–79.

116 / THE COGITO IN HUSSERL'S PHILOSOPHY

————. "La Phénoménologie d'Edmund Husserl il y a trente ans: Souvenirs et réflexions d'un étudiant de 1909." *RIP*, I, No. 2 (January 15, 1939), 366–73.
Ludwig Landgrebe. "Husserls Phänomenologie und die Motive zu ihrer Umbildung." *RIP*, I, No. 2 (January 15, 1939), 277–316.
Paul L. Landsberg. "Husserl et l'idée de la philosophie." *RIP*, I, No. 2 (January 15, 1939), 317–25.
Gerhard Lehmann. *Die Ontologie der Gegenwart in ihren Grundgestalten*. Halle: Niemeyer, 1933. 42 pp.
W. P. Montague. "Concerning Husserl's Phenomenology." *JP*, XXXVI, No. 9 (1939), 232.
Andrew D. Osborn. "A Philosopher's Philosopher." *JP*, XXXVI, No. 9 (1939), 234–36.
H. J. Pos. "Phénoménologie et Linguistique." *RIP*, I, No. 2 (January 15, 1939), 354–65.
Kwan Sakazaki. "Comportement naturel et comportement philosophique" (Japanese text). *Tetsugakuronso* (collection of philosophical dissertations). Tokyo, January, 1937.
Jean-Paul Sartre. "Structure intentionnelle de l'Image." *RMM*, XLV, No. 4 (October, 1938), 543–609.
————. "Une Idée fondamentale de la 'Phénoménologie' de Husserl: l'Intentionnalité." *NRF*, LII, No. 304 (January 1, 1939), 129–32.
Charles Serrus. "Le Conflit du logicisme et du psychologisme." *EP*, II, No. 1 (May, 1928), 9–18.
————. "Catégories grammaticales et catégories logiques." *EP*, III, No. 1 (June, 1929), 20–30.
————. "L'Oeuvre philosophique d'Edmund Husserl." *EP*, IV, No. 1 (May, 1930), 42–46; IV, No. 2–3 (December, 1930), 126–33; V, No. 1 (January–March, 1931), 18–23.
————. "Edmund Husserl: 'Nachwort zu meinen *Ideen*'; Edmund Husserl: *Méditations cartésiennes*." *EP*, V, No. 3 (July–September, 1931), 127–31.
Herbert Spiegelberg. "Der Begriff der Intentionalität in der Scholastik, bei Brentano und bei Husserl." *Philosophische Hefte*, V, No. 1 (1936), 75–91.
Jules Tannery. *Science et Philosophie*. Paris: Alcan, 1912. 336 pp.
S. Vanni-Rovighi. "Il Valore della fenomenologia: A proposito di una discussione promossa dalla Société thomiste." *Rivista di filosofia neo-scolastica* (Milan), XXV, No. 3 (August, 1933), 338–45.

————. "Edmund Husserl." *Rivista de filosofia neo-scolastica* (Milan), XXX, No. 3 (May, 1938), 338–40.
H.-J. de Vleeschauwer. "La Philosophie contemporaine et le criticisme kantien." *EP*, XI, No. 3–4 (December, 1937), 9–14; XII, No. 1–2 (April, 1938), 29–31.
A. de Waelhens. "Descartes et la pensée phénoménologique." *Revue néoscolastique de philosophie* (Louvain), XLI (November, 1938), 571–89.

III. Books and Articles in French Dealing with Husserl and with Husserl's Phenomenology.

Edmund Husserl's transcendental phenomenology has practically not been studied in France, although the *Cartesian Meditations,* which presents its essential theses, has been published in French. A bibliography limited to the narrow range of our study would thus be of little interest. But, as a whole, Husserl's philosophy is not so well known in our country that it would not be useful to include some critical notes on what has been published in French concerning it.

We think it necessary, however, to recall how careful Husserl was, during the last years of his life, to warn his readers against all the interpretations of his work based on the *Logische Untersuchungen* or even against the *Ideen* being taken too literally, as if they definitively established the theses of phenomenology.

I. General Studies on Husserl and on His Phenomenology

1. E. Levinas. *La Théorie de l'intuition dans la phénoménologie de Husserl.* Paris: Alcan, 1930. 223 pp.
This is the most important general study we possess in France on Husserl's philosophy. The author has the merit of basing his analyses, beginning with Chapter II, on the essential theory of the absolute primacy of consciousness and of distinguishing Husserl's intentional idealism from all psychological idealism. He nevertheless does present most of Husserl's logical or epistemological theories; this makes his work extremely thorough, but it makes his analyses a trifle awkward.

The theory of phenomenological reduction and that of constitution are not accorded here a development corresponding to their importance, but we must remember that Levinas' study is prior to the *Cartesian Meditations.*

Levinas reproaches Husserl for not having sufficiently taken into account "man's historical situation" (p. 220); he also sees in the Husserlian primacy of theory a narrowness of phenomenology. This criticism goes farther than Levinas seems to believe: "to complete" phenomenology by eliciting a "richer notion of existence than presence before a contemplating consciousness" (p. 192) does not continue Husserl's effort; rather, it profoundly modifies its direction.

2. "La Phénoménologie." *Journées d'études de la Société thomiste*. Juvisy, September 12, 1932. 135 pp. Juvisy and le Saulchoir: Société thomiste, 1932.

The colloquium summarized here was composed of two meetings. In the first meeting Father Feuling studies phenomenology in itself, by carefully distinguishing Husserl's position from that of Heidegger. Those participating in the discussion include: Noël, Stein, Maritain, Rosenmoeller, de Bruyne, von Rintelen, Söhngen, Devivaise, and Mager.

In the second meeting Father Kremer presents a paper on "A Comparison of Phenomenology and Thomism." Here he emphasizes the interest of the theory of the *Wesensschau* and the Husserlian refutation of naturalism. Discussion: Koyré, Delannoye, Forest, de Bruyne, E. Stein, Söhngen, Kremer. The letters of Buadin and Mazzantini are included as an appendix.

3. Emile Bréhier. *Histoire de la philosophie*. Paris: Alcan, 1926–30. 2 vols. 791 and 1184 pp.

Bréhier presents, in Volume II, *La Philosophie moderne* (pp. 1110–16), the Husserlian critique of psychologism and the theory of intentionality in a particularly clear fashion. In connection with this, he emphasizes an important aspect of phenomenology which is not always noticed: evidence is not conceived here as a criterion of truth which would give us an infallible guarantee against error (p. 1110). Bréhier quite precisely characterizes the *Wesensschau* and the "placing in brackets." He does not attack transcendental phenomenology but remarks that phenomenology remains open: "The *Ideen* are . . . a preface to a philosophy that has not yet been written" (p. 1115).

4. Jean Hering. *Phénoménologie et philosophie religieuse: Etude sur la théorie de la connaissance religieuse*. Studies on history and religious philosophy published by the Faculty of Protestant Theology of the University of Strasbourg. Paris: Alcan, 1926. 148 pp.

The author deplores religious philosophy having become first a philosophy of religion, then a psychology of religion. Phenomenology seems to him to provide the means to transcend this psychologism. This is why he presents its essential theories in the second part of his book (pp. 32–86: "The Phenomenological Movement").

Hering clarifies well the intuitional and resolutely nonconstructive character of phenomenology; he clearly describes the *Wesensschau* and notes what separates Bergson from Husserl. We will make some reservations, however, about his interpretation of intentionality and about the way he understands immanence and transcendence in Husserl's phenomenology. Hering does not accept without qualification the transcendental idealism of the *Ideen*.

Jean Hering. "Phénoménologie et philosophie religieuse." *Revue d'histoire et de philosophie religieuse*, VI, No. 1 (January–February, 1926), 73–79.

The author here summarizes and presents the work mentioned above.

5. Georges Gurvitch. "La Philosophie phénoménologique en Allemagne. I. Edmund Husserl." *Revue de métaphysique et de morale*, XXV, No. 4 (1928), 553–97; reprinted as Chapter 1 in the following work.

Georges Gurvitch. *Les Tendances actuelles de la philosophie allemande*. Paris: Vrin, 1930. 235 pp.

Gurvitch, who specifies quite successfully the similarities and the differences between Bergsonism and phenomenology, first notes the anticonstructive and antisubjectivist character of phenomenology. He then groups under the general heading of "phenomenological reduction" the different Husserlian types of reduction. In his study of intentionality, he insists on the role of attention and thus risks keeping the theory of intentionality on the level of psychology.

There are noticeable differences between the article in the *Revue de métaphysique* and the first chapter of the book on *Les Tendances actuelles de la philosophie allemande*. In the latter, the terminology is somewhat modified (Gurvitch will say *Je* instead of *Moi*); notes and paragraphs are added (for example, pp. 53–57, the paragraph on "the idea of transcendental phenomenology and the last phase of the development of Husserlian thought").

6. Charles Serrus. "L'Oeuvre philosophique d'Edmund Husserl." *Les Etudes philosophiques* (official publication of the Société d'Etudes Philosophiques de Marseille), IV, No. 1 (May, 1930), 42–46; IV, No. 2–3 (December, 1930), 126–33; V, No. 1 (January–March, 1931), 18–23.

In reference to the *Formale und transzendentale Logik* and in order to explain its origin, Serrus retraces the development of phenomenological philosophy, preoccupied as it is with pure logic and finding its unity in the logical problem. The author particularly stresses the theory of the *Erlebnis*, the semiological relation between the intention of meaning and the corresponding realization, and the nature of the *Wesensschau*. He shows the intellectual character of Husserlian intuition. He criticizes the idea of pure logic and thinks that Husserl "followed the mistaken orientation of Kantianism" (third article, p. 23).

The aspects of phenomenology to which Husserl attached the greatest importance during his final years (phenomenological reduction and reflection upon the transcendental "I") are scarcely mentioned. These studies, however, are prior to the *Cartesian Meditations;* Serrus' analysis of them is indicated below (No. 34).

7. Emmanuel Levinas. "Sur les *Ideen* de M. E. Husserl." *Revue philosophique*, CVII (March–April, 1929), 230–65.

A faithful and objective analysis of Husserl's book; the article follows the divisions of the work.

8. B. Groethuysen. *Introduction à la pensée philosophique allemande depuis Nietzsche.* Paris: Stock, 1926. Chapter on Husserl, pp. 88–103.

The author stresses Husserl's desire to escape relativism and to found philosophy "as a rigorous science." He then seeks to present in a simple and accessible manner what phenomenological intuition purports to be. He perhaps gives it a slightly Bergsonian tint.

9. Emile Bréhier. *Histoire de la philosophie allemande.* 2d rev. ed. Paris: Vrin, 1933. 186 pp.

One part (pp. 168 f.) is dedicated to Husserl's antipsychologism and to his *Logical Investigations*, where mathematical judgment is presented as analytic and where syllogistic classical logic appears as a particular case of the general theory of reason. Another part (pp. 175 f.) indicates the descriptive character of phenomenology and summarizes the theory of eidetic intuition.

10. Jean Hering. "La Phénoménologie d'Edmund Husserl il y a trente ans: Souvenirs et réflexions d'un étudiant de 1909." *Revue internationale de philosophie*, I, No. 2 (January 15, 1939), 366–73.

The author describes the feeling of liberation experienced by students coming into contact with phenomenology; its methods allowed them to avoid the limitations of both psychology and positivism.

11. "Husserl." (Obituary notice.) *Revue de métaphysique et de morale*, XLV, No. 3 (1938), supplement, pp. 33–34.

The author (anonymous) indicates the importance of the notion of intentionality in phenomenology and specifies the trans-worldly character of consciousness.

II. Husserl's Rationalism

12. Léon Chestov. "Memento mori: A propos de la théorie de la connaissance d'Edmund Husserl." *Revue philosophique*, CI (January–February, 1926), 5–62.

Husserl's philosophy expresses a deep faith in reason. Man has the right to require that any proposition that purports to be true be rationally justified; evidence is in no sense a mystical voice, and before it the freedom of the mind remains entire.

This position is interesting because of its rigor. Husserl indeed sees that one must choose between wisdom and reason. He opts for the latter and wants philosophy to be a rigorous science. Husserl's reasoning cannot be attacked, and the conflict must be abandoned if we remain on his territory. But one can leave this territory and deliberately enter irrational metaphysics: "as long as logic reigns, the path to metaphysics is barred" (p. 55).

13. Jean Hering. "Sub specie aeterni: Réponse à une critique de la philosophie de Husserl." *Revue d'histoire et de philosophie religieuse* (published by the Faculty of Protestant Theology of the University of Strasbourg) VII, No. 4 (July–August, 1927), 351–64.

There is, in Husserl, a wisdom which is not opposed to reason, but which expresses it. The awakening Chestov speaks of, and to which he invites us, does not concern the phenomenologist but solely the man in the world. How, on the other hand, can one speak of rationalist "prejudice" in connection with a philosophy that is mistrustful of any theory and that wants to be docile about the original character of any new intuition?

14. Léon Chestov. "Qu'est-ce que la Vérité? (Ontologie et éthique)." *Revue philosophique*, CIII (January–February, 1927), 36–74.

Chestov defends his position against Hering's critique (the article, mentioned in No. 13, had been sent to Chestov before its publication, but, because of unfortunate circumstances, it appeared only after Chestov's reply).

The author wonders whether, by placing Husserl under the protection of the idea of eternity, one is not submitting him to the wisdom he wanted to replace with a rigorous rationalism. For, indeed, the choice must be made, and Husserl is interesting only because he creates a philosophy of option and not a philosophy of conciliation. The article ends with considerations on wisdom in Spinoza and in Plotinus.

15. Benjamin Fondane. *La Conscience malheureuse.* Paris: Denoël & Steele, 1936. 307 pp.

Chapter IV (pp. 93–118) is entitled: "Edmund Husserl et l'oeuf de Colomb du Réel." From a perspective analogous to that of Chestov, the author criticizes the Husserlian pretension of seeking an absolute justification for philosophical propositions, whereas existence and reality perhaps clash with it. Husserl is the most characteristic representative of rational intellectualism that Fondane combats and one whose "evidences" most irritate the author.

16. Paul-L. Landsberg. "Husserl et l'idée de la philosophie." *Revue internationale de philosophie*, I, No. 2 (January 15, 1939), 317–25.

Husserl's rationalism, which manages to grasp neither the original character of history nor the intimacy of personal life, could in no way be the philosophy of our time, anxious to meditate on existence. There is, however, more "existential fidelity" in Husserl's life than in the romantic writings of certain fashionable writers.

III. Philosophy of Arithmetic

17. Jules Tannery. *Science et philosophie.* Paris: Alcan, 1912. 336 pp.

The *Philosophie der Arithmetik* is analyzed on pages 79–87. Tannery is particularly concerned here with the idea of equality. He thinks he sees in Husserl a reduction of arithmetic to simple calculus and is astonished by this. Perhaps this conveys Husserl's interest, manifest from the beginning, in the notion of symbol.

IV. Critique of Psychologism

18. Victor Delbos. "Husserl: Sa critique du psychologisme et sa conception d'une logique pure." Lecture given at the Ecole des Hautes Etudes sociales, reprinted in *Revue de métaphysique et de morale,* XIX, No. 5 (1911), 685–98.

This study also composes Chapter II of the following work.

Ch. Andler, V. Basch, J. Benrubi, C. Bougle, V. Delbos, G. Dwelshauvers, B. Groethuysen, H. Norero. *La Philosophie allemande au XIXᵉ siècle.* Paris: Alcan, 1912. 255 pp.

A very clear, very exact exposition of the Husserlian critique of psychologism. Volume I of the *Logische Untersuchungen* forms the essential subject of the study. It seems to us excessive, however, to say that phenomenology sanctions the primacy of logic over psychology, since, from the first edition on, pure phenomenology is presented as a "neutral" investigation, destined to found both psychology and logic (*Logische Untersuchungen,* 1st ed., Vol. II, p. 4).

19. Charles Serrus. "Le Conflit du logicisme et du psychologisme." Paper delivered before the Société d'Etudes Philosophiques in Marseilles, January 26, 1928, and published in *Les Etudes philosophiques,* II, No. 1 (May, 1928), 9–18.

The author concisely, yet clearly, presents the essential features of Husserl's antipsychologism. Although using in particular the *Logische Untersuchungen,* he shows all that separates Husserl from classical ontology. Those who participated in the discussion at this meeting include: Berger, Bourgarel, Rimbaud. Augier and Paliard sent written observations.

20. Charles Serrus. *Le Parallélisme logico-grammatical.* Paris: Alcan, 1933. 514 pp.

Paragraph two of Chapter V is devoted to the relations between pure logic and pure grammar in Husserl's philosophy (pp. 339–81). Serrus thinks that Husserl is dealing with an impoverished logic, that he creates for himself a false idea of grammar, and that he ends in an artificial semiological relation.

21. L. Noël. "Les Frontières de la logique." *Revue néo-scolastique de philosophie,* XVII, No. 66 (May, 1910), 211–33.

The author opposes to psychologism—presenting its tenets with great clarity—Husserl's critique; to him, this position seems not very different from that of Scholasticism. He does indeed see that phenomenology wants to be the foundation for both logic and psychology.

22. Albert Spaier. *La Pensée concrète: Essai sur le symbolisme intellectuel.* Paris: Alcan, 1927. 447 pp.

Section 8 of Chapter I is devoted to Husserl's logicism and to his antipsychologism (pp. 40–42). Spaier attributes to Husserl the opinion according to which logic would be the exclusive science of thought. The allusions Spaier makes to phenomenology are directed more to the psychologists of the Würzburg school than to Husserl.

V. Pure Thought

23. Maurice Pradines. *Philosophie de la sensation. I. Le Problème de la sensation.* Paris: Les Belles Lettres, 1928. 280 pp.

One page (p. 11) on Husserl's intuitive method. Some remarks on the psychologists of Würzburg, who seek, inspired by Husserl's concepts, purity of thought in a meaning which would go beyond any psychological experience.

24. Albert Burloud. *La Pensée d'après les recherches expérimentales de H. J. Watt, de Messer et de Bühler.* Paris: Alcan, 1927. 189 pp.

The author does not directly study Husserl's concepts, which did not influence Watt, and which, if they did act upon Messer and Bühler, did not always inspire them successfully (p. 12).

The relations between thought and language were studied by Husserl as a logician and not as a psychologist.

VI. *Intentionality and Intentional Psychology*

25. Jean-Paul Sartre. "Une Idée fondamentale de la phénoménologie de Husserl: L'Intentionnalité." *Nouvelle revue française*, LII, No. 304 (January 1, 1939), 129–32.

The author stresses the importance and the originality of the theory of intentionality in Husserl.

26. Jean-Paul Sartre. *L'Imagination*. Paris: Alcan, 1936. 163 pp.

Theories of the image can be reduced to three fundamental types, which will be found in a relatively pure state in Descartes, Leibniz, and Hume. Sartre wants to remain on the level of psychology. Yet, in spite of metaphysics, it must be acknowledged that, "between the image and perception, there is a difference of nature" (p. 91). Many difficulties will arise as a result of an eidetic analysis of the image, initiated by Husserl and outlined by the author, who reserves its development for a later time.

27. Jean-Paul Sartre. "Structure intentionnelle de l'image." *Revue de métaphysique et de morale*, XLV, No. 4 (October, 1938), 543–609.

The author denounces in Hume "the illusion of immanence," which has been more or less adopted by many psychologists and philosophers, and according to which the image is in consciousness. He thinks, on the contrary, that the image is a certain manner of "relating to" an object, in which consciousness posits its object as nothingness by way of a content that is not given in-itself but that is the "analogous representative of the object sighted" (p. 608).

This study is not of a historical nature; rather, here we see Sartre applying his personal research to the process of eidetic analysis and to the theory of the intentionality of consciousness borrowed from Husserl. He shows their fruitfulness by contributing, through them, to the elucidation of the "meaning" of the image.

28. Yanne Feldman-Comiti. "Structures intellectuelles: Introduction à l'étude phénoménologique de l'image. A propos d'un ouvrage récent." *Revue de métaphysique et de morale*, XLIV, No. 4 (October, 1937), 767–79.

The work analyzed is Sartre's study on the imagination (No. 26, above). Feldman-Comiti grants him the merit of having shown, in accordance with Husserl, that the image is not *in* consciousness, that it is "a synthetic act and not an element, however fluid one might wish, of a synthesis" (p. 778).

29. Albert Burloud. *La Pensée conceptuelle*. Paris: Alcan, 1927. 412 pp.

In Husserl, intentionality has no properly psychological sense (pp. 45, 251–54, 378). Husserl's transcendent object evokes the thing-in-itself in the eyes of Burloud, who wants solely to describe the psychological phenomenon of the intention.

VII. Grammar and Linguistics

See above: Charles Serrus (No. 20).

30. Charles Serrus. "Catégories grammaticales et catégories logiques." Paper delivered on February 14, 1929, before the Société d'Etudes Philosophiques de Marseille, published in *Les Etudes philosophiques*, III, No. 1 (June, 1929), 20–30.

Study of the relations between grammar and logic in light of the theory of intentionality and the Husserlian conception of the *Erlebnis*. Included in the discussion: Berger, Deshays, Hervé, Nayrac, Paliard.

31. H. J. Pos. "Phénoménologie et linguistique." *Revue internationale de philosophie*, I, No. 2 (January 15, 1939), 354–65.

Husserl has shown that there is a "primitive" knowledge that is at once reality and consciousness. It precedes science; it is even at the basis of any scientific knowledge. Pos illustrates this theme through considerations of linguistic knowledge and primitive linguistic consciousness, which is relatively easily studied retrospectively, starting with practical science as effectively realized, but which is more fruitful if grasped at its origin, beginning at the true beginning, as phenomenology invites us to do.

VIII. Religious Philosophy

See above: Jean Hering (No. 4).

IX. *Transcendental Phenomenology*

32. Jean-Paul Sartre. "La Transcendance de l'Ego: Esquisse d'une description phénoménologique." *Recherches philosophiques*, VI (1936–37), 85–123.

The author wants to show that the ego "is neither formally nor materially *in* consciousness; it is outside, *in the world*" (p. 85). By affirming its transcendency, he in no way wants to make it an absolute; indeed, on the contrary: it is a constituted reality, a being of the world, an object. Sartre agrees with Husserl in making the physical and psychophysical self a transcendent object (p. 87), but he thinks that phenomenological reduction leaves us confronting an impersonal "transcendental field." Husserl, on the contrary, believes in the reality of the transcendental "I," the structure of absolute consciousness.

Sartre's remarkable study seems to us to bear on an essential point. Husserl, who repeats so insistently that the transcendental must not be confused with the psychological, does not always separate the two domains with sufficient clarity. In contrast to Kant, Husserl does not introduce the "I" in order to unify consciousness. Sartre deduces from this that the transcendental "I" has no reason to exist.

We would be less categorical. With Sartre we think that phenomenology has no need of an "I" who realizes the synthetic unity of apperception. But can it do without a center of vision, a point of view? Husserl's interest in Leibnizian monadology, the place the notion of horizon takes in his last published writings, would support this interpretation. All that Sartre says concerning the ego should, it seems, be maintained and its importance preserved, but it is solely the psychic ego that he transforms."

33. Jacques Maritain. "Notes sur la connaissance." *Rivista di filosofia neo-scolastica*, XXIV, No. 1 (January, 1932), 13–23.

The author criticizes the "neo-Cartesian" position taken by Husserl in the *Cartesian Meditations*. He sees in this a return to Kant and to idealism and reproaches him for having separated, from the beginning and in an abusive fashion, the object from the thing. The conclusion of the article criticizes idealism in general.

34. Charles Serrus. "Edmund Husserl—'Nachwort zu meinen *Ideen*'; Edmund Husserl—*Méditations cartésiennes*." *Les*

Etudes philosophiques, V, No. 3 (July–September, 1931), 127–31.

Serrus studies the movement from regional ontologies to transcendental subjectivity and signals the particular difficulties in the ultimate *Wesensschau* that the ego presents to us. Then he objectively summarizes the five Cartesian Meditations. The importance he attaches to the notion of *Erlebnis* leads Serrus to see in transcendental phenomenology a not very coherent mixture of Bergson and Descartes.

X. Historical Comparisons

35. Gaston Berger. "Husserl et Hume." *Revue internationale de philosophie*, I, No. 2 (January 15, 1939), 342–53.

The curious Husserlian idea of "primary givens" which are not psychological facts or subjective constructions, or irrational elements, or absurd things-in-themselves can be clarified by a study of the relations between Husserl and Hume. If phenomenology is set in opposition to Hume's philosophy, it is because it has passed through Hume and because it too has known how to push doubt to its farthest limits. It has well understood that everything is subjective, but, supported by Descartes, it has known how to see in transcendental subjectivity the origin of objectivity itself.

36. J. Marechal. "Phénoménologie pure ou Philosophie de l'action?" *Festschrift für Jos. Geyser*, I (Regensburg, 1931), 377–444.

The author confronts Husserlian phenomenology with Maurice Blondel's philosophy, which seems to him to be broader and more comprehensive. Indeed, he states, "Husserl's severe intellectualism—a Cartesianism purged of all ontological remains—does not lead us to our aim, which is metaphysics" (p. 394).

37. A. de Waelhens. "Descartes et la pensée phénoménologique." *Revue néo-scolastique de philosophie*, XLI (November, 1938), 571–89.

Four pages are devoted to the relations between Descartes and Husserl, who wants, in short, to create a philosophy that is "more Cartesian than that of Descartes" (p. 574). The remainder of the article opposes Descartes and Heidegger and, in particular, Descartes and Jaspers.

38. H.-J. de Vleeschauwer. "La Philosophie contemporaine et le criticisme kantien." Paper delivered before the 1ᵉʳ Congrès national des sociétés françaises de Philosophie (Marseille, April 19, 1938); text published in *Les Etudes philosophiques*, XI, No. 3–4 (December, 1937), 9–14. Discussion in *Les Etudes philosophiques*, XII, No. 1–2 (April, 1938), 29–31.

De Vleeschauwer studies the relations of Kant with Husserl, Nicolaï Hartmann, and Scheler. Phenomenology and critical philosophy are animated by completely different attitudes, and Husserlian intuition is "incompatible with Kant's transcendental method" (p. 10). In spite of this, he judges that "Husserl has taken up the formulation of the question just as Kant had presented it" (p. 10). In the discussion, de Vleeschauwer notes that "the phenomenological doctrine was not created in function of Kant, but rather of positivism" (p. 30).

39. Gaston Berger. "Quelques aspects de la philosophie allemande contemporaine." Paper delivered before the Société d'Etudes philosophiques de Marseille, May 16, 1936, and published in *Les Etudes philosophiques*, X, No. 3–4 (December, 1936), 68–74.

The author examines the principles at the base of logical empiricism, of existential philosophy, and of Husserl's phenomenology. He shows that the three schools are equally concerned with the investigation of meaning and indicates that one can find in Husserl an intellectual method of deliverance. Two letters of Emmanuel Leroux and Charles Serrus accompany Berger's presentation.

40. Fritz Heinemann. "Les Problèmes et la valeur d'une phénoménologie comme théorie de la réalité. Etre et apparaître. Fragment d'introduction à une phénoménologie concrète." Paper delivered before the IXᵉ Congrès international de Philosophie (Paris, 1937). *Actes du Congrès*, X (Paris, 1937), 64–71.

Husserl, Scheler, and Heidegger are united in a common intention: that of making explicit the connections between being and appearance. But this basic preoccupation is masked, in each of them, by accessory questions which prevent it from being adequately treated.

41. G. Gurvitch. "Phénoménologie et criticisme." *Revue philosophique*, CVIII (September–October, 1929), 235–84.

We mention this article, which in itself is quite important, only to avoid confusion. It is not a question there, as one would be led to believe, of the relation of Kant and Husserl but (as its subtitle indicates) of a confrontation between the two movements as they are expressed in the philosophies of Emile Lask and Nicolaï Hartmann.

Appendix

Appendix: Bibliography of Gaston Berger

Compiled by G. Varet

BOOKS

Recherches sur les conditions de la connaissance. Essai d'une théorétique pure. Paris: Presses Universitaires de France, Bibliothèque de philosophie contemporaine, 1941. 195 pp.

Le Cogito dans la philosophie de Husserl. Paris: Aubier, Philosophie de l'esprit, 1941. 159 pp. 2d ed., 1950.

Traité pratique d'analyse du caractère. Paris: Presses Universitaires de France, 1950. XX + 251 pp.; 3d ed., 1955. (Collection "Caractères, I.")

Questionnaire caractérologique. Paris: Presses Universitaires de France, 1950. 16 pp. 2d ed., 1951. 3d ed., 1954. (Collection "Caractères, I.")

Caractère et personnalité. Paris: Presses Universitaires de France, 1954. 110 pp. 2d ed., 1956. (Collection "Initiation philosophique.")

L'Homme moderne et son éducation. Edited, with an introduction, by Edouard Morot-Sir. Paris: Presses Universitaires de France, 1962. 368 pp.

This bibliography appeared originally in *Les Etudes philosophiques*, Vol. XVI, No. 4 (1961). It is included here by permission of the Presses Universitaires de France, who also recently supplied the list of translations of Berger's works into foreign languages, now appearing at the end of the bibliography.

Phénoménologie du temps et prospective. Edited, with a fore-word, by Edouard Morot-Sir. Paris: Presses Universitaires de France, 1964. 278 pp.

PREFACES

Jérôme Casablanca. *La Sélection éducative.* Preface by Gaston Berger. Paris-Marseille, 1945. 216 pp.
L'Enseignement universitaire et la gestion de l'entreprise. Paris: A.F.A.P., 1957. 218 pp. ("Etudes et témoignages," p. 3).
La Prévision et le contrôle de gestion, by J. Aubert-Krier, J. Benoit, R. B. Thibert. Journées d'études of 20–21 January 1956 organized by the Institut d'Administration des Entreprises de Rennes. Preface by Gaston Berger. Rennes: Centre régional d'études et de formation économique (Impr. réunies), 1957. (Bibliothèque d'Administration des entreprises.)

ARTICLES IN JOURNALS AND IN COLLECTIONS

"Esthétique et histoire de la philosophie dans la pensée de J. Segond." *Les Etudes philosophiques,* XI, No. 1–2 (1937), 28–33.
"Husserl et Hume." *Revue internationale de philosophie,* I, No. 2, (1939), 342–53.
"Le Progrès de la réflexion chez Bergson et chez Husserl." *Hommage à Bergson.* Neuchâtel: La Baconnière, 1941.
"Les Thèmes principaux de la phénoménologie de Husserl." *Etudes de métaphysique et de morale* (1944), 23–43.
"Léon Brunschvicg moraliste." *Revue de métaphysique et de morale,* L, No. 2 (1945), 116–26 (special number devoted to Léon Brunschvicg).
"Pour un cinquantenaire: Hommage à Maurice Blondel. La cohésion architecturale de la doctrine de M. Blondel, Pensée, Vie et Réalité sous une même médiation unifiante." *Les Etudes philosophiques* (1945).
"La Cohésion architecturale de la pensée de M. Blondel: Hommage à Maurice Blondel." *Cahiers de la nouvelle journée.* Paris: Bloud & Gay, 1946.
"Valeur pratique d'une philosophie de l'absolu." *Les Etudes philosophiques* (December, 1946), 190–96.
"The Different Trends of Contemporary French Philosophy." *Philosophy and Phenomenological Research,* VII (1946).

"Qu'est-ce que la philosophie?" *Revue de synthèse* (1947).

"Qu'est-ce que la métaphysique?" *Giornale di metafisica*, II (September, 1947), 320–29.

"Puissance et liberté." *Les Etudes philosophiques*, III, No. 2 (1947), 120–25 (special number for the Amsterdam Congress).

"Der Mensch und die Metaphysik." *Blick in die Wissenschaft* (Berlin), I, No. 4 (1948), 20–27.

"La 'philosophie de l'esprit' de Léon Brunschvicg." *Giornale di metafisica*, I (1949), 20–27.

"Existentialism and Literature in Action: Two Lectures on Present-Day Problems in France." *University of Buffalo Studies*, XVIII, No. 4 (December, 1948), 157–86.

"L'Aventure humaine." *Estudios franceses*. Mendoza, 1949.

"Expérience et transcendance." Pp. 96–112 in *La Philosophie française: L'Activité philosophique en France et aux Etats-Unis*, Vol. II. Ed. Marvin Farber. Paris: Presses Universitaires de France, 1950. (Published simultaneously in English by the University of Buffalo.)

"Psychology in France Today." *French Bibliographical Digest.* New York: United States Embassy, Cultural Services Department, 1950. V + 95 pp.

"En hommage à Maurice Blondel." *Les Etudes philosophiques*, V, No. 1 (1950), 5–7.

"Pour un retour à Descartes." *Les Etudes philosophiques*, V, No. 2 (1950), 156–64.

"La Crisis morale de tiempo presente." *Annales de l'université de Santiago* (1951).

"La Enseñanza de la filosofia en la Universidad." *La Universidad en el siglo XX*. Lima, 1951.

"Louis Lavelle." *Les Etudes philosophiques*, VI, Nos. 2–3 (1951), 123–27.

"Le Temps et la participation dans l'œuvre de Louis Lavelle." *Giornale di metafisica*, VII (1952), 451–60.

"La Philosophie de John Dewey." *Les Etudes philosophiques*, VII, Nos. 1–2 (1952), 5–15.

"Le Temps chez Anouilh." *Les Etudes philosophiques*, VII, No. 3 (1952), 243–50.

"Témoignages sur Maurice Blondel." *Les Etudes philosophiques*, VII, No. 4 (1952), 313–15. (Introduction to the number devoted to the Journées blondéliennes d'Aix, December, 1952.)

"French Philosophy: Contemporary France." *The Culture of*

France in Our Time. New York: Buffalo University Press, 1954.
"L'Originalité de la phénoménologie." *Les Etudes philosophiques*, IX, No. 3 (1954), 249–59.
"L'Homme et la technique." *L'Encyclopédie française*, Vol. XIV: *La Civilisation quotidienne*. Paris, 1954.
"La Signification humaine de la recherche scientifique." *La Nef* (1954).
"La Vocation dans la philosophie de René Le Senne." *Giornale di metafisica*, X, No. 3 (1955), 390–97.
"De la contradiction à l'inspiration: Etude sur la philosophie de R. Le Senne." *Les Etudes philosophiques*, X, No. 3 (1955), 420–27 (number devoted to René Le Senne).
"L'Avenir des sciences de l'homme." *La Nef* (1956), p. 13.
"L'Esthétique théâtrale." In *Création et vie intérieure: Recherches sur les Sciences et les Arts: Mélanges offerts à Georges Jamati*. Paris: Editions du C.N.R.S., 1957.
"Sciences humaines et prévision." *La Revue des deux mondes*, February 1, 1957.
Introduction to the section "Philosophie." *L'Encyclopédie française*, Vol. XIX: *Philosophie et religion* (1957).
"La Phénoménologie transcendentale." *L'Encyclopédie française*, Vol. XIX.
Introduction to the section "Religion." *L'Encyclopédie française*, Vol. XIX.
"La Vie mystique." *L'Encyclopédie française*, Vol. XIX. (Reprinted in *Prospective*, No. 7.)
Foreword. *L'Encyclopédie française*, Vol. XI: *La Vie internationale* (1957).
Foreword. *L'Encyclopédie française*, Vol. XII: *La Chimie* (1958).
Preface: "L'Attitude prospective." *Prospective*, No. 1 (May, 1958).
"Humanisme et technique." *Revue de l'enseignement supérieur*, III, No. 1 (1958), 5–10.
"Hommage à Arnold Reymond." *Revue de philosophie et théologie* (Lausanne), IX (1959), 41–43.
"Caractère et liberté." *Les Etudes philosophiques*, XIV, No. 1 (1959), 47–52 (number on "Liberty").
Foreword. *L'Encyclopédie française*, Vol. XX: *Le Monde en devenir* (1959).
"L'Inquiétude contemporaine." *L'Encyclopédie française*, Vol. II.

"Quelques caractéristiques générales du monde actuel." *L'Ency-clopédie française*, Vol. XX.
"Le Temps." *L'Encyclopédie française*, Vol. XX. (Reprinted in *Prospective*, No. 7.)
"L'Attitude prospective." *L'Encyclopédie française*, Vol. XX.
"L'Education dans un monde d'accélération." *L'Encyclopédie française*, Vol. XX.
"En guise de conclusion: Civilisations et cultures." *Prospective*, No. 3, "Rapports de l'Occident avec le reste du monde." Paris: Presses Universitaires de France, 1959.
"Culture, qualité, liberté," *Prospective*, No. 4 (November, 1959).
"Enseignement et recherche." *Revue de l'enseignement supérieur*, V, No. 3 (1960), 5–10. (Reprinted in *Prospective*, No. 7.)
Foreword. *L'Encyclopédie française*, Vol. IX: *L'Univers économique et social* (1960).
"L'Oeuvre collective, le projet, la fonction d'arbitre." *l'Encyclopédie française*, Vol. IX.
Foreword. *L'Encyclopédie française*, Vol. IV: *La Vie* (1960).
"En guise de conclusion: Le problème des fins." *Prospective*, No. 5, "Le Progrès scientifique et technique et la condition de l'homme" (1960), 125–35.
"En guise d'avant-propos: Méthodes et résultats." *Prospective*, No. 6 (1960), 1–14.

COMMUNICATIONS

"La Philosophie critique de Spir." Société d'études philosophiques de Marseille, 1927. (Résumé: *Bulletin de la Société d'études philosophiques du Sud-Est*, I [1927], 25–27. Discussion: M. Blondel, J. Segond, H. Claparède-Spir.)
"La Psychologie et la pratique." Société d'études philosophiques de Marseille, 1928. (Résumé: *Bulletin de la Société d'études philosophiques du Sud-Est*, II [1928], 78–79. Discussion: R. Bourgarel, M. Blondel, M. Foucault, A. Hesnard, E. Souriau, pp. 79–95.)
"Remarques sur la connaissance." Société d'études philosophiques de Marseille, meeting of 21 March 1929. (Résumé: *Les Etudes philosophiques*, III [1929], 83–84. Discussion: M. Blondel, Léon Brunschvicg, C. A. Emge, R. Le Senne, P. Montagné, J. Paliard, Ch. Serrus, Gustave-A. Monod, R. Bourgarel, pp. 84–100.)

"La Morale et les affaires modernes." Société lyonnaise de philosophie, 20 June 1929. (Résumé: *Les Etudes philosophiques,* IV [1930], 1–4. Discussion: Mme. Waltz, M. Carlhian, M. Beau, M. Lachièze-Rey, pp. 5–6.)

"Empirisme et transcendance." Société d'études philosophiques de Marseille, meeting of 16 May 1931, and Société lyonnaise de philosophie, meeting of 11 June 1931. (Résumé: *Les Etudes philosophiques,* VI [1932], 1–3. Discussion: M. Blondel, L. Brunschvicg, J. Chevalier, J. Darbon, J. Delvové, C.-A. Emge, Ed. Goblot, P. Lachièze-Rey, R. Le Senne, J. Maréchal, E. Souriau, J. Segond, J. Paliard, Gustave-A. Monod, pp. 3–19.)

"L'Idéalisme de Descartes." Société de philosophie de Toulouse, April, 1932. (Cf. *Les Etudes philosophiques,* VII [1933], 57; résumé by G. Bastide.)

"Existence et réalité." Société de philosophie de Bordeaux, 1935. (Unpublished?)

"Quelques aspects de la philosophie allemande contemporaine." Société d'études philosophiques de Marseille, meeting of 16 May 1939. (Résumé: *Les Etudes philosophiques,* pp. 68–73. Letters by Emm. Leroux, Ch. Serrus, pp. 73–74.)

First Congress of the Sociétés françaises de philosophie, organized by Gaston Berger. Marseilles, 21–23 April 1938. (Cf. *Les Etudes philosophiques,* XI, Nos. 3–4 [1937], and XII, Nos. 1–2 [1938].)

"L'Idée d'univers." *Travaux du IIe Congrès national des Sociétés de philosophie françaises et de langue française* (Lyon, 13–15 April 1939), published under the auspices of the Société lyonnaise de philosophie. Lyon: Neveu, 1939.

"Connaissance de la Nuit; saint Jean de la Croix." Société d'études philosophiques de Marseille, meeting of 6 March 1943. (Résumé in *Les Etudes philosophiques,* XVII and XVIII (1943–44), 43–46. Letter of J. Paliard, pp. 47–48.)

"La Connaissance des hommes." Sociétés d'études philosophiques de Marseille, meeting of 11 December 1943. (Résumé: *Les Etudes philosophiques,* XVII and XVIII [1943–44], 58–60.)

"Commémoration de Léon Brunschvicg." Introductory address by G. Berger. Sociétés de philosophiques de Marseille, meeting of 3 December 1944. (Published in *Les Etudes philosophiques,* XX [1945], 4–6.)

"Métaphysique et psychologie." Société d'études philosophiques de Marseille, meeting of 19 May 1945. (Résumé: *Les Etudes philosophiques,* II [1946], 44–45.)

"Existence et rationalité." Congrès international de philosophie (Rome), 1946. (Résumé: *Atti del Congresso internazionale di Filosofia* [sponsored by the Instituto di Studi filosofici; Rome, 15–20 November 1946]; Vol. II: *L'Esistenzialismo* [Milan: Castellani, 1948].)

"L'Epanouissement des valeurs." Société d'études philosophiques de Marseille, meeting of 25 January 1947. (Résumé: *Les Etudes philosophiques*, II [1947], 72–73.)

"Structure et épanouissement des valeurs." *Les Valeurs. Actes du III⁰ Congrès des Sociétés de philosophie de langue française* (Brussels). Louvain: Nauwelaerts; Paris: Vrin, 1947.

"L'Homme et les systèmes." *Bibliothèque du X⁰ Congrès international de philosophie* (Amsterdam, 1948). Amsterdam: North-Holland Publishing Co., 1949.

"La Philosophie et la société." *Actas del Primer Congresso Nacional de Filosofia*, I, 505–14. Mendoza (Argentina): Universidad Nacional de Cuyo, 1949.

"Les Discussions des philosophes." *Actas del Primer Congresso Nacional de Filosofia*, II, 878–83. Mendoza (Argentina): Universidad Nacional de Cuyo, 1949.

"L'Homme et ses limites." *Actas del Primer Congresso Nacional de Filosofia*, II, 968–73. Mendoza (Argentina): Universidad Nacional de Cuyo, 1949.

"La Liberté et le temps." *La Liberté. Actes du IV⁰ Congrès des Sociétés de philosophique de langue française*. Neuchâtel: La Baconnière, 1949.

"Recherches phénoménologiques sur le temps." Société de philosophie de Bordeaux, April 1950. (Text: *Bulletin de la Société de philosophie de Bordeaux*, No. 27 [1950].)

"Approche phénoménologique du problème du temps." Société française de philosophie, meeting of 3 June 1950. (*Bulletin de la Société française de philosophie*, XLIV, [1954], 89–132. Discussion: Bénézé, Bréhier, Koyré, Lalande, A. Leroy, Le Senne, E. Minkowski, Polin, M. Souriau, E. Wolff. Letters by Bréhier, Minkowski, Paliard, Segond.)

"L'Homme prométhéen." Congrès international de philosophie, Lima, 1951.

"Mort et mémoire." Congrès international de philosophie, Lima, 1951.

"Mémoire et retention." V⁰ Congrès des Sociétés de philosophie de langue française, Bordeaux, September, 1950. (Text: *Bul-*

letin de la Société de philosophie de Bordeaux, V [1950], 14–17.)

"Le Temps de l'action." VI° Congrès des Sociétés de langue française, Strasbourg, 10–14 September 1952. (Text: *L'Homme et l'histoire,* pp. 67–71. Paris: Presses Universitaires de France, 1952.)

"L'Homme en situation." Société d'études philosophiques de Marseille, meeting of 21 March 1953. (Résumé: *Les Etudes philosophiques,* VIII [1953], 92–93.)

"Le Message philosophique de Jacques Paliard." Société d'études philosophiques de Marseille, meeting of 16 November 1954. (Cf. *Les Etudes philosophiques,* X [1955], 138.)

"La Psychologie du peintre." Société française d'esthétique, Paris, 1954. (Text: *Revue d'esthétique,* VII [1954], 198–204.)

"Léon Brunschvicg." VII° Congrès des Sociétés de philosophie de langue française, Grenoble, 12–16 September 1954. (Résumé: *La Vie, la pensée.* Paris: Presses universitaires de France, 1954.)

"Structures psychologiques et situations humaines fondamentales." In: *Centre économique et social de perfectionnement des cadres,* 2d Session, 1953–54, Cycle 2A: *Relations humaines.* Paris: Fédération nationale des Syndicats d'Ingénieurs et Cadres supérieurs, 1955.

"Introduction psychologique et philosophique aux problèmes du fédéralisme." Inaugural lecture at the Centre de science politique de l'Institut d'études juridiques de Nice, 1954. In: *Le Fédéralisme,* pp. 11–29. Paris: Presses Universitaries de France, Bibliothèque des Centres d'études spécialisés, 1956.

"L'Opinion publique, phénomène humain." Inaugural lecture at the Centre de science politique de l'Institut d'études juridiques de Nice, 1955. In: *L'Opinion publique,* pp. 11–23. Paris: Presses Universitaires de France, 1957.

"Le Chef d'entreprise: Philosophe en action." Lecture delivered to the General Studies section of the Centre de recherche et d'étude des chefs d'entreprise, 8 March 1955. (Extracts in: *Prospective,* No. 7, pp. 47–66.)

"L'Homme et ses problèmes dans le monde de demain. Essai d'anthropologie prospective." Société d'études philosophiques de Marseille, meeting of 8 November 1955. (Résumé: *Les Etudes philosophiques,* XI [1956], 150–51.)

"Le Problème des choix: Facteurs politiques et facteurs techniques." Concluding remarks to the third meeting of the Centre

de science politique de Nice, 1956. In: *Politique et technique,* III, 370–82. Paris: Presses Universitaries de France, Bibliothèque des Centres d'études spécialisés, 1958.
"Du prochain au semblable." VIII° Congrès des Sociétés de philosophie de langue française, Toulouse, September, 1956. (Text: *La Présence d'autrui.* Toulouse: Privately published, and Paris: Presses Universitaires de France, "La nouvelle recherche," No. 12 [1957].)
"Recherches sur la phénoménologie du temps." Institut supérieur de philosophie de Louvain, 6 November 1956. (Cf. *Les Etudes philosophiques,* XII [1957], 112.) (Unpublished.)
"Notice sur la vie et les travaux de René Le Senne, 1888–1954." Institut de France, Académie des Sciences morales et politiques. Paris: Imprimerie de Firmin Didot, 1956.
"Hommage aux philosophes aixois." Inaugural address, IX° Congrès des Sociétés de philosophie de langue française, 2 September 1957. (Text: *Les Etudes philosophiques,* XIII [1958], 115–22.)
"Hommes politiques et chefs militaires: Etude psycho-sociologique." Opening address to the fourth session of the Centre de science politique de Nice, 1957. In: *La Défense nationale,* IV, 15–29. Paris: Presses Universitaires de France, Bibliothèque des Centres d'études spécialisés, 1958.
"Psychologie des relations internationales." Lecture given at the fifth session of the Centre de science politique de Nice, 1958. In: *Les Affaires étrangères,* V, 145–49. Paris: Presses Universitaires de France, Bibliothèque des Centres d'études spécialisés, 1959.
"Médecine et culture d'Extrême-Orient." Address for the opening of the Exposition de la Médecine en Extrême-Orient, Paris, 4 October 1959. (Text: *Prospective,* No. 7, pp. 79–87.)
"Hommage à Bergson." Final session of the Congrès Bergson, Grand Amphithéâtre de la Sorbonne, 19 May 1959. (Text: *Bulletin de la Société française de philosophie,* LIV [1960], 21–26.)
"L'Idée d'avenir et la pensée de Teilhard de Chardin." Lecture given at the Clermont-Ferrand theater, 6 May 1960, at the invitation of the Cercle Marcel Proust. (Text: *Prospective,* No. 7, pp. 131–52.)
"Juges, avocats, plaideurs, accusés: Notes psychologiques." Lecture given at the Centre universitaire méditerranéen de Nice, 19 July 1960. (Text: *Prospective,* No. 7, pp. 31–45.)

"Textes de Gaston Berger. Hommage à Gaston Berger." *Prospective*, No. 7 (1961), pp. 31–152. (For details, see above, *passim*.)

DISCUSSIONS

[Unless otherwise indicated, all discussions occurred at meetings of the Société d'Etudes philosophiques de Marseille and were subsequently published in *Les Études philosophiques* (abbreviated *EP*). Entries appear in chronological order.]

Etienne Souriau. "L'Identité." May 24, 1927. *EP*, II (1928), 83–84.

Gustave Monod. "L'Objet de la psychologie." December 8, 1927. *EP*, II (1928), 92–93.

Jacques Paliard. "Le Refus de l'alternative chez Paul Valéry." December 23, 1927. *EP*, II (1928), 7–8.

Charles Serrus. "Le Conflit du logicisme et du psychologisme." January 26, 1928. *EP*, II (1928), 12–14.

Henri Hurtin. "Le Problème de la peine de mort." March 22, 1928. *EP*, II (1928), 68–69.

Etienne Souriau. "Esthétique et construction du moi." December 14, 1929. *EP*, IV (1930), 26.

Jacques Paliard. "Recherche sur la pensée implicite." April 5, 1930. *EP*, IV (1930), 106.

A. Durand. "La Psychologie animale." May 31, 1930. *EP*, IV (1930), 124–25.

Charles Baudouin. "L'Art et la psychanalyse." November 24, 1930. *EP*, V, 6–7.

P. E. Vial. "Les Facteurs psychologiques de la pensée idéaliste." February 28, 1931. *EP*, V, 59.

P. Padova. "Réflexions sur la science moderne." March 31, 1931. *EP*, V, 113–16.

H. Hurtin. "Les Conditions de la persuasion." November 21, 1931. *EP*, 22–23.

Richard P. McKeon. "La Philosophie et l'action." *Bulletin de la Société française de philosophie*, XLV, (1951), 93–129. (Discussion: Berger, Bréhier, Lavelle, Lenoir, A. Leroy.)

Journées cybernétiques, Gaston Berger presiding, March 24–25, 1956. *EP*, XI (1956), 376–78.

Alfred J. Ayers. "La Mémoire." (Meeting of 1 December 1956.) *Bulletin de la Société française de philosophie*, 1957, 161–224.

(Discussion: Berger, Goldmann, A. Leroy, Ohana, Poirier, Ruyer, Wahl, Wolff.)

Roger Caillois. "Problèmes du rêve." (Meeting of 25 May 1957.) *Bulletin de la Société française de philosophie*, LI (1957), 105–44. (Discussion: Berger, Auger, J. d'Ormesson, Patri, Wolff, J. Brun, J. Wahl, et al.)

ADDRESSES

"Commémoration de Léon Brunschvicg: Allocution de Gaston Berger." *Les Etudes philosophiques*, I (1945), 4–6.

Université d'Aix-Marseille, "Rentrée solennelle." November 23, 1945. Marseille: Impr. marseillaise, 1945. Addresses by M. le recteur Gau, and by MM. Martel, Henri Fluchère, and Berger.

"Cérémonie commémorative en l'honneur du centenaire de Henri Moissan, 1852–1907." Paris, Maison de la Chimie, May 20, 1958. Paris: Impr. Chaix, 1953. Addresses by G. Berger, P. Lebeau, Jean Gall.

Institut international de philosophie, Meetings at Varsovie. "Les Rapports de la pensée et de l'action," July 17–26, 1957, opening session, address of the vice-president. Wroclaw-Warszawa: Zaklad narodowy Imienia ossolinskich, 1958. (Zeszyty problemeowe nauki polskiej, XV.)

"Bergson et nous." *Actes du X⁰ Congrès des Sociétés de philosophie de langue française* (Paris, May 17–19, 1959). (Discussions, *Bulletin de la Société française de philosophie*.) Paris: Armand Colin, 1960. Inaugural address of the president of the Congress.

International Institute of Philosophy and Indian Philosophical Congress, meetings at Mysore, India, August 29–31, 1959. "Traditional Cultural Values, East and West." Address by the president of the Institute.

BOOK REVIEWS

[Unless otherwise indicated, all reviews appeared in *Les Etudes philosophiques*.]

I. Kant. *Kritik der reinen Vernunft*. Ed. Raymond Schmidt. Leipzig: F. Meiner, 1929. *EP*, I, No. 1 (1927), 13.

Theodor L. Haering. *Ueber Individualität in Natur und Geisteswelt*. Leipzig: Teubner, 1927. *EP*, I, No. 2 (1927), 56–57.

Dr. A. Hesnard. *La Vie et la mort des instincts.* Paris: Stock, 1926. *Ibid.,* pp. 57–58.

August Messer. *Einführung in die Erkenntnistheorie.* 3d ed. Leipzig: F. Meiner, 1927. *Ibid.,* p. 59.

Heinrich Schmid. *Philosophisches Wörterbuch.* Leipzig: A. Kröner, 1922. *Ibid.,* p. 60.

Auguste Valensin. *L'Essence de la théorie de la science.* Archives de philosophie, 1926. *Ibid.*

Max Walleser. *Die Sekten des alten Bouddhismus.* Heidelberg: Winter, 1927. *Ibid.,* p. 61.

Edmond Goblot. *La Logique des jugements de valeur.* Paris: A. Colin, 1927. *EP,* I, No. 3 (1927), 115–17.

Karl Vorländer. *Geschichte der Philosophie.* 7th ed. Leipzig: F. Meiner, 1927. *Ibid.,* p. 121.

E. Augier. *Une Psychologie objective est-elle possible?* Paris: Alcan, 1928. *EP,* II, No. 1 (1928), 12–14.

M. Foucault. *Cours de psychologie,* Vol. II. Paris: Alcan, 1928. *Ibid.,* pp. 30–31.

Edmond Goblot. "Le Réel." *Revue de l'Université de Bruxelles,* I (1927). *Ibid.,* pp. 33–34.

A. Hesnard. "L'Individu et le sexe." Paris: Stock, 1927. *Ibid.,* pp. 34–35.

Maurice Maeterlinck. *La Vie de l'espèce.* Paris: Carpentier, 1928. *Ibid.,* p. 37.

Georges Politzer. *Critique des fondements de la psychologie.* Paris: Rieder, 1928. *Ibid.,* pp. 40–42.

Ernest Seillière. *Morale et religions nouvelles en Allemagne.* Paris: Payot, 1927. *Ibid.,* pp. 43–44.

Paul Archambault. *Vers un réalisme intégral.* Paris: Bloud & Gay, 1928 (Cahiers de la Nouvelle Journée). *EP,* II, No. 2 (1928), 104–6.

Jacques Durand-Doat. *Le Sens de la métaphysique* and *Essai sur l'étendue.* Paris: Vrin, 1928. *Ibid.,* pp. 111–13.

Heinrich Ratke. *Systematisches Lexikon zu Kants Kritik der reinen Vernunft.* Leipzig: F. Meiner, 1929. *Ibid.,* p. 116.

Franziska Baumgarten. *Die Berufseignungsprüfung.* Munich: Oldenburg, 1928. *EP,* III, No. 1 (1929), 36–37.

C. E. Emge. *Die philosophische Gestalt der religiösen Dogmatik.* Munich: Reinhardt, 1929. *Ibid.,* pp. 43–44.

C. A. Emge. *Hegels Logik und die Gegenwart.* Karlsruhe: G. Braun, 1927. *Ibid.,* pp. 44–45.

Heinrich Gomperz. *Platons Selbstbiographie.* Berlin: W. de Gruyter, 1928. *Ibid.,* p. 45.

Maxime Leroy. *Descartes, le philosophe au masque.* Paris: Rieder, 1928. *Ibid.,* p. 47.

J. P. Nayrac. *Science, morale, progrès.* Paris: Vrin, 1928. *Ibid.,* p. 49.

Louis F. Anderson. *Das Logische, seine Gesetze und Kategorien.* Leipzig: F. Meiner, 1929. *EP,* III, No. 2–3 (1929), 122.

Joan Avinyo-Andreu. *Moderna visio del Lullisme.* Barcelona: Impr. de La Casa P. Caritat, 1929. *Ibid.,* pp. 122–23.

Hans Driesch. *Grundprobleme der Psychologie.* 2d ed. Leipzig: Emm. Reinicke, 1929. *Ibid.,* pp. 126–27.

Hans Leisegang. *Deutsche Philosophie in XX. Jahrhundert.* Breslau: F. Hirt, 1928. *Ibid.,* pp. 130–31.

Erwin Metzke. *Karl Rosenkranz und Hegel.* Leipzig: W. Helms, 1929. *Ibid.,* p. 132.

Eugenio Rignando. *Problèmes de psychologie et de morale.* Paris: Alcan, 1928. *Ibid.,* pp. 134–35.

Charles Serrus. *L'Esthétique transcendantale et la science moderne.* Paris: Alcan, 1929. *Ibid.,* pp. 135–38.

L. Baudry. *Petit traité de logique formelle.* Paris: Vrin, 1929. *EP,* IV, No. 1 (1930), 49.

Festschrift Edmund Husserl zum 70 Geburtstag gewidmet. Halle: Niemeyer, 1929. *Ibid.,* pp. 51–53.

Leibniz. *Discours de métaphysique,* ed. Henri Lestienne. Paris: Vrin, 1929. *Ibid.,* p. 53.

J. Maréchal. *Au seuil de la métaphysique: Abstraction ou intuition.* Louvain: Institut supérieur de philosophie, 1929. *Ibid.,* pp. 57–58.

Heinrich Staubinger. *Einführung in die Religionsphilosophie.* Freiburg im Breisgau: Herder, 1929. *Ibid.,* pp. 60–61.

J. Tricot. *Traité de logique formelle.* Paris: Vrin, 1930. *Ibid.,* p. 61.

Maurice Blondel. *Une Enigme historique: Le Vinculum substantiale.* Paris: Beauchesne, 1930. *EP,* IV, No. 2–3 (1930), 141–43.

Rudolf Carnap. *Abriss der Logistik.* Vienna: J. Springer, 1929. *Ibid.,* p. 145.

Jacques Durand-Doat. *La Question ultime.* Paris: Vrin, 1930. *Ibid.,* pp. 146–48.

G. Gurvitch. *Les Tendances actuelles de la philosophie allemande.* Paris: Vrin, 1930. *Ibid.,* pp. 150–52.

Joseph Maréchal. *Phénoménologie pure ou philosophie de l'action: Festgabe Joseph Geyer.* Regensburg: J. Habbel, 1930. *Ibid.,* p. 154.

Mary Evelyn Clarke. *A Study in the Logic of Value.* London: University of London Press, 1929. *EP,* V, No. 1 (1931), 25–26.

E. Levinas. *La Théorie de l'intuition dans la phénoménologie de Husserl.* Paris: Alcan, 1930. *Ibid.,* pp. 30–32.

Emile Lubac. *Les Niveaux de conscience et d'inconscient.* Paris: Alcan, 1929. *Ibid.,* pp. 32–33.

Désiré Roustan. *La Culture au cours de la vie.* Paris: Institut Pelman, 1930. *Ibid.,* pp. 35–36.

Marie Collins Swabey. *Logic and Nature.* New York: University Press, 1930. *Ibid.,* pp. 37–39.

Erich Adickes. *Kants Lehre von der doppelten Affektion unseres Ich.* Tübingen: Mohr, 1929. *EP,* V, No. 2 (1931), 85–86.

Ernst Benz. *Das Todesproblem in der stoischen Philosophie.* Stuttgart: Kohlhammer, 1929. *Ibid.,* p. 86.

René Le Senne. *Le Devoir.* Paris: Alcan, 1931. *Ibid.,* pp. 91–95.

Maurice Simart. *Interprétation du monde moderne.* Paris: Flammarion, 1930. *Ibid.,* p. 99.

African Spir. *Propos sur la guerre.* Paris: Truchy-Leroy, 1930. *Ibid.,* pp. 99–100.

Studies in the Nature of Truth. Berkeley: University of California Press, 1929. *Ibid.,* pp. 100–101.

Charles Baudouin. *Mobilisation de l'énergie.* Paris, 1931. *EP,* V, No. 3 (1931), 121–22.

Marcel Boll and André Boll. *L'Art contemporain.* Paris: Delagrave, 1931. *Ibid.,* pp. 123–24.

Léon Brunschvicg. *De la connaissance de soi.* Paris: Alcan, 1931. *Ibid.,* pp. 124–25.

René Le Senne. *Le Mensonge et le caractère.* Paris: Alcan, 1930. *Ibid.,* pp. 135–37.

Martin Scheerer. *Die Lehre von der Gestalt.* Berlin: W. de Gruyter, 1931. *Ibid.,* pp. 138–40.

Julien Benda. *Essai d'un discours cohérent.* Paris: Gallimard, 1931. *EP,* VI, No. 1 (1932), 37–39.

Marcel Boll. *Qu'est-ce que: Le hasard, l'énergie, etc.* Paris: Larousse, 1931. *Ibid.,* p. 39.

Léon Brunschvicg. *Pascal.* Paris: Rieder, 1932. *EP,* VI, No. 2–3 (1932), 88–89.

Jean Delvové. *Réflexions sur la pensée comtienne.* Paris: Alcan, 1932. *Ibid.,* pp. 91–93.

Marcel Foucault. *Premières leçons de psychologie expérimentale.* Paris: Delagrave, 1930. *Ibid.,* p. 94.

Pierre Lachièze-Rey. *L'Idéalisme kantien.* Paris: Alcan, 1931. *Ibid.,* pp. 96–98.

D. Parodi. *Du positivisme à l'idéalisme.* Paris: Vrin, 1930. *Ibid.,* pp. 99–100.

J. Segond. *La Sagesse cartésienne et la doctrine de la science.* Paris: Vrin, 1932. *Ibid.,* pp. 102–5.

Gaston Bachelard. *Le Pluralisme cohérent de la chimie moderne.* Paris: Vrin, 1932. *EP,* VII, No. 1–2 (1933), 62–64.

Marcel Foucault. *La Mesure de l'intelligence chez les écoliers.* Paris: Delagrave, 1933. *Ibid.,* pp. 67–68.

Robert Heiss. *Logik des Widerspruchs.* Berlin: W. de Gruyter, 1932. *Ibid.,* pp. 68–69.

Hans Reichenbach. *La Philosophie scientifique,* trans. Vuillemin. Paris: Hermann, 1932. *Ibid.,* pp. 71–72.

J. Segond. *La Vie de Spinoza.* Paris: Perrin, 1933. *Ibid.,* pp. 72–73.

Jean Wahl. *Vers le concret.* Paris: J. Vrin, 1932. *Ibid.,* pp. 74–75.

Walter Blumenfeld. *Sinn und Unsinn.* Munich: Reinhardt, 1933. *EP,* VII, No. 3–4 (1933), 144.

La Phénoménologie. Le Saulchoir, 1933. *Ibid.,* p. 153.

Arnold Reymond. *Les Principes de la logique.* Paris: Boivin, 1933. *Ibid.,* pp. 154–55.

Emile Bréhier. *Histoire de la philosophie allemande.* 2d ed. Paris: Vrin, 1933. *EP,* VIII, No. 1–2 (1934), 40–41.

Léon Brunschvicg. *Les Ages de l'intelligence.* Paris: Alcan, 1934. *Ibid.,* pp. 41–42.

Eugen Fink. "Was will die Phänomenologie Husserls," *Die Tatwelt* (1934). *Ibid.,* pp. 44–45.

Reinhardt Kynast. *Logik und Erkenntnistheorie der Gegenwart.* Berlin: Junger & Dünnhaupt, 1930. *Ibid.,* p. 47.

Louis Lavelle. *La Présence totale.* Paris: Aubier, 1934. *Ibid.,* pp. 48–49.

Charles Serrus. *Le Parallélisme logico-grammatical.* Paris: Alcan, 1933. *Ibid.,* pp. 50–52.

J. Vialatoux. *Philosophie économique.* Paris: Desclée de Brower, 1933. *Ibid.,* pp. 53–54.

Siegfried Weinberg. *Erkenntnistheorie.* Berlin: Carl Heymanns, 1930. *Ibid.,* p. 55.

Rudolf Zocher. *Husserls Phänomenologie und Schuppes Logik.* Munich: E. Reinhardt, 1932. *Ibid.,* pp. 55–56.

148 / APPENDIX

Henri Delacroix. *Les Grandes formes de la vie mentale.* Paris: Alcan, 1934. *EP*, VIII, No. 3–4 (1934), 112.
Max Diez. *Sprachen, Denken, und Erkennen.* Berlin: W. de Gruyter, 1934. *Ibid.*, pp. 112–14.
Hans Hahn. *Logik, Mathematik und Naturerkennen.* Vienna: Gerold, 1933. *Ibid.*, p. 117.
Wilhelm Kopelmann. *Logik.* Berlin: Pan-Verlag, 1933. *Ibid.*, p. 118.
Joseph Maréchal. *Précis d'histoire de la philosophie moderne.* Louvain: Museum Lessianum, 1933. *Ibid.*, pp. 123–24.
Otto Neurath. *Einheitswissenschaft und Psychologie.* Vienna: Gerold, 1933. *Ibid.*, pp. 124–25.
Moritz Schlick. *Les Enoncés scientifiques.* Paris: Hermann, 1934. *Ibid.*, pp. 125–26.
Maurice Blondel. *La Pensée.* 2 vols. Paris: Alcan, 1934. *EP*, IX, No. 1–2 (1935), 32–40.
Rudolf Carnap. *L'Ancienne et la nouvelle logique,* trans. Vuillemin. Paris: Hermann, 1933. *Ibid.*, p. 57.
René Descartes. *Lettres sur la morale,* ed. J. Chevalier. Paris: Boivin, 1934. *Ibid.*, pp. 60–61.
Louis Fondard. *Essai sur la signification psychique du milieu.* Marseille: Ged, 1934. *Ibid.*, pp. 61–62.
Charles Serrus. *La Méthode de Descartes et son application à la métaphysique.* Paris: Alcan, 1933. *Ibid.*, pp. 73–74.
Maurice Caullery. *Les Conceptions modernes de l'hérédité.* Paris: Flammarion, 1935. *EP*, IX, No. 3–4 (1935), 154.
Hermann Glockner. *Hegel Lexikon.* Leipzig: Fromanns Verlag, 1934. *Ibid.*, pp. 161–62.
Arrigo Levasti. *Mistici del duecento.* Milan: Rizzoli, 1935. *Ibid.*, pp. 166–67.
Werner Illeman. *Husserls vor-phänomenologische Philosophie.* Leipzig: S. Hirzel, 1932. *EP*, X, No. 1–2 (1936), 46–47.
Jacques Paliard. *Connaissance de l'illusion.* Paris: Bloud & Gay, 1936. *Ibid.*, pp. 49–51.
Friedrich Weidauer. *Kritik der Transzendental-Phänomenologie Husserls.* Leipzig: Hirzel, 1933. *Ibid.*, pp. 52–53.
André Cresson. *La Représentation.* Paris: Boivin, 1936. *EP*, X, No. 3–4 (1936), 100–101.
Georges Dumas. *Nouveau Traité de Psychologie.* Paris: Alcan, 1936. *Ibid.*, p. 101.
J. Hessing. *Das Selbstbewusstwerden des Geistes.* Stuttgart: Frommans, 1936. *Ibid.*, p. 105.

I. Kant. *Opus postumum*. Ed. A. Buchenau. Berlin: W. de Gruyter, 1936. *Ibid.*, p. 105.

Karl Popper. *Logik der Forschung*. Vienna: Julius Springer, 1935. *Ibid.*, pp. 111–12.

Emile Bréhier. *La Philosophie au Moyen Age*. Paris: Albin Michel, 1937. *EP*, XI, No. 1–2 (1937), 46–48.

Léon Brunschvicg. *Descartes*. Paris: Rieder (Maîtres de la littérature), 1937. *Ibid.*, pp. 48–49.

"Descartes, Troisième centenaire 1937. Recueils d'études sur Descartes." *Ibid.*, pp. 52–53.

Jean Fiolle. *La Crise de l'humanisme*. Paris: Mercure de France. *Ibid.*, pp. 53–55.

Georges Le Roy. *La Psychologie de Condillac*. Paris: Boivin, 1937. *Ibid.*, pp. 60–61.

Armand Petitjean. *Imagination et réalisation*. Paris: Denoël & Steele, 1936. *Ibid.*, pp. 68–69.

Oskar Philippe. *Le Réalisme absolu*. Metz: Cahiers de Nouménologie, 1937. *Ibid.*, pp. 69–70.

J.-P. Sartre. *L'Imagination*. Paris: Alcan (N.E.P.), 1936. *Ibid.*, pp. 70–71.

Takiyettin Temulrap. *Ueber die Grenzen der Erkennbarkeit bei Husserl und Scheler*. Berlin: Verlag für Staatswissenschaften und Geschichte. *Ibid.*, pp. 74–75.

Etienne Souriau. *Avoir une âme: Essai sur les existences virtuelles*. Paris: Les Belles-Lettres (Annales de l'Université de Lyon, 3d ser., fasc. 5), 1938. *EP*, XIV (1940), 43–44.

Jacques Paliard. *Le Théorème de la connaissance*. Paris: Aubier, 1938. *Ibid.*, pp. 45–47.

Jean Delvové. *De la matière en général*. Paris: Boivin, 1939. *EP*, XV, No. 1–2 (1941), 42–45.

J. Segond. *Hasard et contingence*. Paris: Hermann, 1938. *EP*, XV, No. 3–4 (1941), 78–79.

J. Segond. *La Logique du pari*. Paris: Hermann, 1938. *Ibid.*, pp. 79–80.

René Le Senne. "Introduction à la philosophie," and "Traité de morale générale." The first two treatises in the collection *Logos*. *EP*, XVI, No. 1–4 (1942), 39–45.

Emile Bréhier. *La Philosophie et son passé*. Paris: Presses Universitaires de France (N.E.P.), 1940. *Ibid.*, pp. 54–56.

Pierre Lachièze-Rey. *Les Idées morales, sociales et politiques de Platon*. Paris: Boivin, 1940. *Ibid.*, pp. 61–63.

Jean Laporte. *Le Problème de l'abstraction*. Paris: Presses Universitaires de France, 1940. *Ibid.*, pp. 63–65.

Gabriel Madinier. *Conscience et mouvement*. Paris: Alcan, 1938. *Ibid.*, pp. 68–70.

J. Segond. *Psychologie de Jean Racine*. Paris: Les Belles-Lettres, 1940. *Ibid.*, pp. 70–72.

Charles Serrus. *Essai sur la signification de la logique*. Paris: Alcan (N.E.P.), 1939. *Ibid.*, pp. 72–73.

Etienne Souriau. *L'Instauration philosophique*. Paris: Alcan, 1939. *Ibid.*, pp. 73–76.

Whewell. *De la construction de la science*, ed. R. Blanché. Paris: Vrin, 1938. *Ibid.*, pp. 76–78.

Léon Brunschvicg. *Descartes et Pascal, lecteurs de Montaigne*. Neuchâtel: La Baconnière, 1942. *EP*, XVII–XVIII (1943–44), 68–70.

J. Segond. *Signification de la tragédie*. Paris: Les Belles-Lettres, 1943. *EP*, XX (1945), 54–55.

Marvin Farber. *The Foundation of Phenomenology*. Cambridge: Harvard University Press, 1943. *EP*, I, No. 2, N.S. (1946), 128–32. Also reviewed in *Revue philosophique*, LXXXVIII (1948), 92–95.

David Hume. *Traité de la nature humaine*, ed. André Leroy. Paris: Aubier, 1946. *EP*, I, No. 2 (1946), 155.

Georges Bastide. *Les Grands thèmes moraux de la civilisation occidentale*. Paris: Les Editions françaises nouvelles, n.d. *EP*, I, No. 3–4 (1946), 244.

Etudes de Neuro-psycho-pathologie infantile. Marseille: Comité de l'enfance délinquante, 1946. *Ibid.*, pp. 247–48.

Jeanne Hersch. *L'Etre et la forme*. Neuchâtel: La Baconnière, 1946. *Ibid.*, pp. 249–50.

Josiah Royce. *Philosophie du loyalisme*, trans. J. Morot-Sir. Paris: Aubier, 1946. *Ibid.*, p. 255.

Yves Simon. *Prévoir et Savoir*. Montréal: Editions de l'Arbre, 1944. *Ibid.*, pp. 260–61.

"Paul Valéry vivant." *Cahiers du Sud* (Marseilles) (1946). *Ibid.*, pp. 261–62.

Condillac. *Oeuvres philosophiques*, Part I, ed. G. Le Roy. Paris: Presses Universitaires de France (Corpus général des philosophes français), 1947. *EP*, II, No. 1 (1947), 87.

African Spir. *Principes de justice sociale*. Geneva: Editions du Mont-Blanc, 1945. Hélène Claparède-Spir, *Tolstoï, Nietzsche, Rilke*. Geneva: Georg, 1944. *Ibid.*, pp. 93–94.

Emile Bréhier. *Science et humanisme*. Paris: Albin Michel (Collection Descartes), 1947. *EP*, III, No. 3–4 (1948), 351–52.

Léon Brunschvicg. *Héritage de mots, héritage d'idées*, 1948. *Ibid.*, pp. 353–54.

John F. Callahan. *Fours Views of Time in Ancient Philosophy*. Cambridge: Harvard University Press, 1948. *EP*, IV, No. 1 (1949), 93.

Louis Lavelle. *Introduction à l'ontologie*. Paris: Presses Universitaires de France (N.E.P.), 1947. *Ibid.*, pp. 98–99.

H. A. Wolfson. *Philo*. 2 vols. Cambridge: Harvard University Press, 1947. *Ibid.*, pp. 102–3.

J. M. Bochenski. *Bibliographische Einführungen in das Studium der Philosophie*. Bern: Francke, 1949. *EP*, IV, No. 2 (1949), 213.

James Feibleman. *Introduction to Peirce's Philosophy Interpreted as a System*. New York: Harper & Bros., n.d. *Ibid.*, pp. 213–14.

Georges Poulet. *Etudes sur le temps humain*. Edinburgh: Edinburgh University Press, 1949. *EP*, IV, No. 3–4 (1949), 476–77.

Edmund Husserl. *Gesammelte Werke*, Vols. I and II. The Hague: M. Nijhoff, 1950. *Idées directrices*, trans. P. Ricoeur. Paris: Gallimard; 1950. *EP*, V, No. 2 (1950), 264–65.

Emile Bréhier. *Transformations de la philosophie française*. Paris: Flammarion, 1950. *EP*, V, No. 2 (1950), 362–63.

Etienne Souriau. *Les Deux cent mille situations dramatiques*. Paris: Flammarion, 1950. *EP*, VI, No. 1 (1951), 123–24.

Jean Baruzi. *Création religieuse et pensée contemplative*. Paris: Aubier, 1941. *EP*, VI, No. 2–3 (1951), 229–30.

Emile Callot. *La Renaissance des sciences de la vie au XVIᵉ siècle*. Paris: Presses Universitaires de France, 1951. *Ibid.*, pp. 235–36.

Georges Gusdorf. *Mémoire et personne*. 2 vols. Paris: Presses Universitaires de France, 1951. *Ibid.*, pp. 241–42.

René Le Senne. *La Destinée personnelle*. Paris: Flammarion, 1951. *EP*, VI, No. 4 (1951), 261–66.

De Brie. *Bibliographia philosophica 1934–1945*. Brussels: Spektrum, 1951. *Ibid.*, pp. 372–73.

Raoul Cerighelli. *Bernard Palissy*. Paris: Institut national agronomique, 1951. *Ibid.*, pp. 373–74.

Liliane Guerry. *Cézanne et l'expression de l'espace*. Paris: Flammarion, 1950. *Ibid.*, pp. 375–76.

Kierkegaard. *Diaro*, ed. Cornelio Fabro. 3 vols. Brescia: Morcelliana, 1948–51. *Ibid.*, p. 378.

La Mia prospectiva filosofiaca. Padua: Ed. Liviana, 1950. *Ibid.*, pp. 378–79.
Thomas Munro. *The Arts and Their Interrelations.* New York: Liberal Arts Press, 1949. *Ibid.*, pp. 383–84.
Daniel Somer Robinson. *The Principles of Conduct.* New York: Appleton-Century-Crofts, 1951. *Ibid.*, pp. 385–86.
Robert Blanché. *Les Attitudes idéalistes.* Paris: Presses Universitaires de France, 1949. *EP*, VII, No. 1–2 (1952), 143–45.
Jacques Duron. *La Pensée de George Santayana.* Paris: Nizet, 1950. *Ibid.*, pp. 148–50.
Ulysse Filippi. *Connaissance du monde physique.* 2d ed. Paris: Albin Michel, 1952. *Ibid.*, pp. 150–51.
Denise Saada. *Initiation à la psychanalyse.* Paris: Maloine, 1950. *Ibid.*, pp. 166–67.
Morelly. *Code de la nature*, ed. G. Chinard. Paris: R. Clavreuil, 1950. *EP*, VII, No. 4 (1952), 453.
M. F. Sciacca. *In spirito e verità.* Brescia: Morcelliana, 1952. *Ibid.*, p. 454.
Victor Goldschmidt. *Le Système stoïcien et l'idée de temps.* Paris: Vrin, 1953. *EP*, VIII, No. 4 (1953), 437.

STUDIES AND CRITICAL REVIEWS
OF THE WORKS OF GASTON BERGER

Le "Cogito" . . . , 1941.
Anonymous. *Revue de métaphysique et de morale*, 1941, pp. 87–88.
Pierre Lachièze-Rey. *Les Etudes philosophiques*, 1942, pp. 51–54.
Emile Bréhier. *Revue philosophique*, CXXXII (1942–43), 173–76.

Les Conditions de la connaissance, 1941.
Anonymous. *Revue de métaphysique et de morale*, 1941, pp. 85–87.
J. Segond. *Les Etudes philosophiques*, 1941, pp. 64–70.
J. W. *Revue philosophique*, CXXXII (1942–43), 170–72.

Traité pratique . . . , 1950.
M. Gex. *Studia philosophica* (Basel), XI (1951), 244–45.
A. Pinto de Carvalho. *Revista da Faculdade de Letras* (Lisbon), XVII (1951), 26.
D. S. R. *The Personalist*, XXXII (1951), 322.

A. Hayen. *Nouvelle Revue théologique* (Tournai), LXXIV (1952), 323–24.
P. Malrieu. *Journal de psychologie,* XLVI (1953), 255–56.
D. Anzieu. *Revue philosophique,* CXXXIX (1954), 296.
François Gauchet and Roger Lambert. *La Caractérologie d'Heymans et Wiersma: Etude statistique sur le questionnaire de M. Gaston Berger.* Paris: Presses Universitaires de France, 1959. (Collection du Travail humain.)

Caractère et personnalité, 1954.
G. V. *Bibliographie de la philosophie,* I, No. 1 (1954), 33.
G. Blanco. *Sapientia* (La Plata), X (1955), 233.
H. Riefstahl. *Philosophischer Literaturanzeiger,* XII (1959), 23–24.

ARTICLES ON GASTON BERGER

Jacques de Bourbon-Busset. "Gaston Berger." Pp. 5–8 in "Gaston Berger, un philosophe dans le monde moderne," *Prospective,* No. 7. Paris: Presses Universitaires de France, 1961.
Edouard Morot-Sir. "René Le Senne et Gaston Berger." *Ibid.,* pp. 9–18.
Léon Delpech. "Maurice Blondel et Gaston Berger." *Ibid.,* pp. 17–29.
Maurice Bayen. "Gaston Berger (1896–1960)," *Revue de l'Enseignement supérieur,* No. 4 (1960), pp. 5–12.

"Gaston Berger," a special issue of *Les Etudes philosophiques* (Vol. XVI, No. 4, 1961) entirely devoted to Berger, contains the following articles:

Edouard Morot-Sir. "Ascèse philosophique et amitié selon Gaston Berger." Pp. 311–16.
René Lacroze. "Gaston Berger devant le mystère du temps." Pp. 317–26.
Pierre Mesnard. "Gaston Berger et la caractérologie." Pp. 327–37.
Joseph Moreau. "Sagesse de Gaston Berger." Pp. 339–48.
Henry Duméry. "La Théorétique." Pp. 349–62.
Roger Mucchielli. "La Philosophie et la vie." Pp. 363–77.
Gilbert Tournier. "Gaston Berger et la prospective." Pp. 379–88.
Louis Millet. "L'Esprit de la prospective." Pp. 389–92.
Charles Devivaise. "Rencontre avec Gaston Berger." Pp. 393–96.
Marcel Barzin. "Gaston Berger." Pp. 397–99.
Augusto Guzzo. "Gaston Berger et l'Italie." Pp. 401–5.

André Mercier. "Des valeurs du vrai, du beau et du bien." Pp. 407–12.
H. W. Schneider. "Gaston Berger." Pp. 413–15.
Juan Zaragüeta. "Gaston Berger et la pensée espagnole." Pp. 417–18.

TRANSLATIONS INTO FOREIGN LANGUAGES

English   A collection of essays which first appeared in the journal *Prospective*. Soon to be published by Gordon & Breach, Science Publishers, Inc., of New York.

German   *Phénoménologie du temps et prospective.* To be published in 1972 by Schäuble Verlag.

Spanish   *Caractère et personnalité.* Buenos Aires: Paidos.
L'Homme moderne et son éducation. Madrid: Cid.
Traité d'analyse du caractère. Buenos Aires: El Ateneo.

Italian   *Traité d'analyse du caractère.* Turin: Borla.

Portuguese   *Caractère et personnalité.* Lisbon: Uniao Grafica.
Traité d'analyse du caractère. Rio de Janeiro: Agir.

Rumanian   *L'Homme moderne et son éducation.* Bucharest: Editura Didactica si Pedagogica.

Index